[]NCOLN CHRISTIAN COLLEGE AND SEMINARY

Loving Your City into the Kingdom

City-Reaching Strategies for a 21st-Century Revival

Ted Haggard and Jack W. Hayford

Regal

A Division of Gospel Light
Ventura, California, U.S.A.

Published by Regal Books
A Division of Gospel Light
Ventura, California, U.S.A.
Printed in U.S.A.

Regal Books is a ministry of Gospel Light, an evangelical Christian publisher dedicated to serving the local church. We believe God's vision for Gospel Light is to provide church leaders with biblical, user-friendly materials that will help them evangelize, disciple and minister to children, youth and families.

It is our prayer that this Regal book will help you discover biblical truth for your own life and help you meet the needs of others. May God richly bless you.

For a free catalog of resources from Regal Books/Gospel Light please contact your Christian supplier or call 1-800-4-GOSPEL.

Unless otherwise indicated, all Scripture quotations in this book are taken from the *Holy Bible, New International Version®. NIV®.* Copyright © 1973, 1978, 1984 by International Bible Society. Used by permission of Zondervan Publishing House. All rights reserved.

Other versions used are:
KJV—King James Version. Authorized King James Version.
NASB—New American Standard Bible, © 1960, 1962, 1963, 1968, 1971, 1972, 1973, 1975, 1977 by The Lockman Foundation. Used by permission.
NKJV—Scripture taken from the *New King James Version.* Copyright © 1979, 1980, 1982 by Thomas Nelson, Inc. Publishers. Used by permission. All rights reserved.
TLB—Verses marked (*TLB*) are taken from *The Living Bible* © 1971. Used by permission of Tyndale House Publishers, Inc., Wheaton, IL 60189. All rights reserved.

© Copyright 1997 by Ted Haggard and Jack W. Hayford.
All rights reserved.

Library of Congress Cataloging-in-Publication Data
Haggard, Ted.
    Loving your city into the kingdom / Ted Haggard and Jack W. Hayford.
    p.   cm.
    Includes bibliographical references.
    ISBN 0-8307-1895-8 (trade paper)
    1. City missions. 2. Evangelistic work. 3. Interdenominational cooperation. I. Hayford, Jack W. II. Title.
    BV2653.H33 1997   96-52722
    269'.2' 091732—dc21   CIP

2 3 4 5 6 7 8 9 10 11 12 13 14 15 16 /03 02 01 00 99 98

Rights for publishing this book in other languages are contracted by Gospel Literature International (GLINT). GLINT also provides technical help for the adaptation, translation and publishing of Bible study resources and books in scores of languages worldwide. For further information, contact GLINT, P.O. Box 4060, Ontario, CA 91761-1003, U.S.A., or the publisher.

DEDICATION

The ideas for *Loving Your City into the Kingdom* were first planted in my (Ted Haggard) heart by the late missionary to Mexico, Daniel K. Ost.

His ministry became sharply focused after a time of prayer when God allowed him to see Mexico tip on its edge with millions of people falling into hell. Even though this experience was of supreme significance in his life, the intense emotional pain it produced prevented him from articulating the details of the vision.

To see Ost on a platform with Bible in hand, weeping as hundreds of Mexicans surrendered to Christ was a normal occurrence in the latter part of his life.

Daniel Ost's passion for unsaved souls not only led to the formation of the largest residential Bible School in Mexico, but also built huge Faith, Hope and Love Centers that held services every hour from 9:00 A.M. to 10:00 P.M. every day, six days a week, all year.

In these centers, full-time altar workers prayed with respondents to the altar call and, as they finished, another call was given with additional people coming to Christ. These workers led people to Christ all day long, while special Bible and practical living classes were simultaneously being taught. Because the services were scheduled so tightly, the altar-call music for one service became the music for the following service. The flow of people coming and going was constant. The result was a cycle of worshiping, praying, coming to Christ and being discipled—all because of a passion for souls.

Brother Danny, as he was affectionately referred to by the Mexican church, has been home with the Lord since 1985; however, my memories of him praying and crying for Mexico City, Monterrey,

96087

Guadalajara, Puebla, Tampico, San Luis Potosi, Calcutta, New York, Chicago, Bombay, New Delhi and other cities have convinced me that God is in love with the lost within the major cities of the world. Ost often repeated the slogan: "Winning the lost at any cost." And in response to God's call on his life he would say, "If you're called to be a missionary, why stoop to be a king?"

In 1984 just prior to his homegoing, Danny Ost was riding in a car through the countryside north of Colorado Springs. He unexpectedly ordered that the car be stopped, then he jumped out and began walking around a 35-acre field—claiming it for the use of God's kingdom. When he came to the high point on the property, he stopped and prayed that God would build something there to serve the lost of the world. Today, 11 years later, the World Prayer Center is being built on that site.

Because missionary Danny Ost loved the lost, and thus loved the cities of the world, we dedicate this book to his memory.

CONTENTS

Acknowledgments

It takes a team to write this kind of book—and this team has been a great one. From people such as Bill Bright and C. Peter Wagner who have been so generously supportive, to the city strategists associated with NAE and Mission America—especially Reverend Glenn A. Barth, I am immensely grateful for your assistance. To everyone list ed in the table of contents, I give a warm thank-you...for your lives, for allowing His ministry to flow through you, for your authentic love for the lost and for getting your materials to me on time.

A heartfelt thank-you is in order to my wife, Gayle, and our children, Christy, Marcus, Jonathan, Alex and Elliott, who sacrificed family nights so Daddy could write. And to Lance Coles, Coleman Jarrell, Russ Walker, Ross Parsley and the many other ministry-team leaders at New Life Church who pastored and served our church family in the absence of the senior pastor: Job well done.

And to the New Lifers: Tamra Farah, Mark McWilliams, Madalene Harris and staff members such as Ross Parsley, Meg Britton, Paul Jacobson and John Bolin who helped compile and edit these manuscripts.

And certainly, the fine believers at Regal Books, especially my editor, Karen Kaufman, who made this book possible. Thank you...for loving the people of our cities.

Ted Haggard

INTRODUCTION

Christian leaders are now more than ever working *together* to reach the lost. After years of struggle to develop focus within the Body of Christ, the finality of heaven and hell is forcing local church leaders and servant ministries (parachurch ministries) to form partnerships that are producing eternal results.

Globally, Christianity is growing at three times the rate of the world's population, according to missiologiest Jack Dennison from DAWN ministries. Even the most conservative observers report that 30,000 people are coming to Christ daily in both China and India; 10,000 daily in Latin America; and 20,000 daily in Africa. Globally, at least 165,000 people are coming to Christ every single day. Christianity is by far the fastest growing religious group in the world.

But because God loves the lost so much, He is now emphasizing the necessity of strategic praying and planning to ensure that every person on earth has an opportunity to hear and believe the gospel message. A.D. 2000 and Beyond has as its goal "A church for every people and the gospel for every person by A.D. 2000." Intercessors, church planters, Bible distribution ministries and many others are being networked with local churches and servant ministries to fulfill that vision.

We can do this by working *together* as a Body, and responsibly responding to the Master's call to "Love Your City into the Kingdom."

Our responsibility is clearly stated in Ezekiel 3:18,19:

> When I say to a wicked man, "You will surely die," and you do not warn him or speak out to dissuade him from

his evil ways in order to save his life, that wicked man will die for his sin, and I will hold you accountable for his blood. But if you do warn the wicked man and he does not turn from his wickedness or from his evil ways, he will die for his sin; but you will have saved yourself.

Because we hold the message of life, we have worked together as a Body of believers to reach unreached people groups throughout the world. Now, what we have learned to do globally, we are applying locally—in our own cities.

Chapters 1, 2 and 3 show us how to pray together to receive God's vision and mobilize His Body within our cities.

Chapters 4 and 5 offer proven methods for developing a city strategy, ensuring every person within our cities an opportunity to hear the gospel in an understandable way.

Chapters 6 and 7 illustrate various ways to implement our strategy so the available resources within the Body of Christ can be utilized to saturate a community with the gospel.

Chapters 8 and 9 depict the life-giving churches of a city, growing as a result of the united efforts to communicate the gospel.

And chapter 10 demonstrates that it can be done.

Thus, we PRAY TOGETHER,

PLAN TOGETHER,

GO TOGETHER,

and GROW TOGETHER.

When we function like a Body, it works!

PRAY AGAINST THE DESTRUCTION OF THE CITY

THE HOLY SPIRIT'S WAKE-UP CALL

JACK HAYFORD

The brilliant glow on the digital clock at my bedside lit the numerals like a strobe light in the darkness. It wasn't the brightness, but the significance of the *precise* minute on the dial that signaled an alarm to me.

4:44!

It shined—no, it SHOUTED! The indicator stood at the exact minute I (Jack Hayford) had months before offered to God as a means of "calling" me to special middle-of-the-night prayer.

Of course, like any sensitive Christian, I would be willing to rise at *any* time I sensed the grip of the Lord drawing me to prayer. But my sleep patterns had been changing with the onset of my 50s, and I had found myself naturally waking up with an increased frequency.

Because I had long before been convinced of the value of mid-nighttime prayer—both for biblical as well as practical reasons—my more frequent rising had prompted a dilemma. "Lord," I inquired, "am I supposed to pray *every* time I wake up?" Of course, I doubted this was the Father's intent, but at the same time, I wanted to be available to any intercessory purpose He might have for me.

To resolve my question, *and* to indicate my intention to be available to the Holy Spirit for emergency "calls" to prayer, about two years before I had made a prayer covenant with God: "If You, Father, have a special call for me to intercede, to help me differentiate between a 'natural' wake-up call and one *You* intend, please signal me with a wake-up that occurs at this exact time." The "sign" time I requested was 4:44.

Now it had happened. But what made it all the more compellingly dramatic at this moment was that this was the second consecutive morning it had happened! No alarm. No natural explanation: just the silent, glowing numerals.

The day before I had risen immediately, but quietly so as not to disturb my wife's rest. The 4:44 had not been the only start to my soul, but the words that whispered within were even more startling: *Pray against the destruction of the city of Los Angeles.*

As unmistakably clear as the words were, I was somewhat unnerved by them. I was troubled by memories of instances in our city when "warnings" had been issued.

Throughout the years of my pastorate in Los Angeles, I have repeatedly heard of "prophets" who announced dates and times of Southern California's demise—of destruction coming with divine judgment to sink Los Angeles into the Pacific Ocean like Atlantis into the Aegean. The seismic nature and geological volatility of our region provided enough credibility to *any* prognosis of disaster to create an uneasiness, even when the demeanor of the self-declared "voice of God" was obviously a kook.

But now, here *I* was—"hearing voices," and doubly bewildered: first, because I was *not* disposed toward a desire to be the latest on the local list of weirdos; and second, because I *did* sense the genuineness and clarity of the prompting I had received. Still, I was cautious.

A focus had distilled in my mind as I sauntered into our living room in the pre-dawn grayness of that July morning. Still feeling puzzled by the words to pray against the city's destruction, I sat looking out the window onto the backyard lawn. "Lord, I'm here. I'll pray however You direct."

Only moments later my mind reflected on a special report our local newspaper had featured about two weeks before. The reporting team had presented a strategic analysis of what would happen in one highly populated area of our Southland if a magnitude 7.+ earthquake were to strike at five o'clock in the afternoon. The statistical projections were staggering:

- Thousands of people pouring onto the streets from offices just closing would be speared by a rain of shattered glass falling from high-rises.
- Many would be crushed as freeway overpasses pancaked, following the liquefaction of subterranean clay across the basin area.
- At least 150,000 dwellings would be immediately destroyed or burned: mostly due to the unavailability of water as broken pipelines shut off the primary means against fires, which spread rapidly as broken gas lines fed the blaze.
- Emergency vehicles would be paralyzed from reaching scenes of disaster where fire injury or other problems wreaked post-quake havoc.
- Estimated totals between 15,000 and 20,000 would be dead within days, due to immediate death or unattended injuries, assault by looters and vandals or the loss of power that would immobilize hospital functions.

As I reviewed these recollections, I realized that the Holy Spirit intended to use this litany of disaster as a teaching tool. The impression that began to settle over my understanding did not come by a voice. But the clear prayer guidance I was receiving was so specific, it is easiest for me to express as a direct quotation. It was practical and sensible, and further, I could breathe a sigh of relief. Although a compelling urgency accompanied the message, I was relieved to be given a directive anyone could pass on without creating doubt about his or her sanity. I sensed this prompting:

> You are not being told "Los Angeles will be destroyed," because this city is **already** being destroyed. It does not need a catastrophic disaster to experience destruction because the Destroyer is already at work. The toll you have recounted, which a severe earthquake might cost, is small in comparison to the reality that stalks this city every day.
>
> **More** than mere thousands are being speared through by the shafts of hell's darts, seeking to take their souls. **More** than 150,000 homes (not merely houses) are being assailed by the sin and social pressures that rip families and marriages apart.
>
> **More** havoc is being wreaked by the invisible grindings of evil power than tectonic plates could ever generate. A liquefaction of the spiritual foundations that alone allow a society to stand is wiping out the underpinnings of relationships, of righteous behavior and of healthy lifestyle.
>
> You are to pray against **THIS**—the present, ongoing, devastating destruction of the city of Los Angeles.

The force of that morning's wake-up was profound, convincing me that I was to personally pray for my city with a deepened zeal.

MORE SPECIFIC GUIDANCE

But now it was day two.

I could hardly believe the second morning's "call." This had never happened to me before. Even though, since my covenant to get up at 4:44, I had been prompted by this early A.M. call a few times, that this double-barreled-alarm call was too providential to be considered a happenstance. So, this morning, I began to do more than pray as I had the day before: I felt I was to ask the Lord for guidance as to how this prayer call should be applied.

I now recognized that this deepened sense of assignment had implications beyond my personal prayer life. I was being directed to bring a new emphasis to our whole congregation's intercessory mission for our city. That wouldn't be difficult, because a healthy habit of prayer had already been established.

Strong times of intercession, including prayer for our nation, state and city, were not new to our church family. Since 1973, when the Holy Spirit moved upon us through a stirring prophetic "word," a continuing sense of responsibility for sustained intercession has characterized our Wednesday night gatherings. Praiseful worship, focused prayer for our church ministries, prayer-circle sharing of personal concerns and a united time of informed intercession all precede a teaching time in God's Word.

Four-digit attendance figures are the norm on Wednesday, including all department activities—with 600 to 700 adults in the sanctuary on their knees. So a grid of prayer habit already existed, which could readily be tapped into with a new thrust of watch care over Los Angeles.

Now, with the double wake-up call, I began to share the prayer issues the Holy Spirit had defined for me. In my private prayer for the city that first morning, an initial agenda was formulated into an outline. I had not struggled to alliterate—but somehow the Ds framing my prayer list deepened the penetration of the word DESTRUCTION in my soul. Because the Bible reveals the vile ministry of a high-level demon angel name, *Appolyon*, the Destroyer, I sensed a divine targeting for spiritual warfare. I felt that his minions were at work in manifold ways, which the Holy Spirit had helped me to define. I knew we were to pray against:

- **Disease**...because it is always rampant—sickness, affliction, pain (our city is a center of the AIDS epidemic);
- **Depression**...because oppressive presences were everywhere—discouragement, homelessness, poverty (Los Angeles's population is swept with the economic and emotional need consequent to deprived minorities, employment and illegal immigrant problems);
- **Death**...because suicide, murder and hopelessness abound (gang violence and domestic strife add a greater toll to the predictable large number of natural deaths that bring grief to a metropolis);

- **Dissolution**...because of the commonplace practice of dissolving covenants; breaking oaths and violating contracts in personal, business and family relationships (the pressured atmosphere of the big city enhances hell's skill at creating a mindless irresponsibility toward any commitment that appears to get in the way of "quick success" or "instant fulfillment");

- **Disappointment**...for people whose dreams have been shattered or their ideals violated, bringing them to bitterness, cynicism and futility (Hollywood's offer of fame and fortune attracts a constant stream of candidates for wealth and recognition, who only arrive to find heartbreak);

- **Deception**...through error, false counsel and lying spirits that have flourished in the city for many years (the flourishing of New-Ageism and false-science-based cults of humanism and occultism thrive amid the poor and wealthy alike).

With these points of focused intercession as the starting place, I began to lead my flock forward in faithful, compassion-filled prayer for Los Angeles.

Among other things I did was bring teaching based on biblical cases of "prayer for cities," e.g., Abraham's intercession for Sodom, Jeremiah's passionate concern for Jerusalem, Jesus' weeping over that same city, Paul's encounter with the Lord concerning Corinth.

These efforts marked my opening response to those two mornings at 4:44. A few months later, however, an additional directive began to stir my heart. The Holy Spirit moved me to make a "Citywide Prayer" focus at our Pastors Seminar.

TAKING YOUR CITY FOR GOD

For more than 20 years now, our congregation has hosted an interdenominational conference for pastors and spiritual leaders each November. This three-and-one-half-days event takes a distinct theme each year. I not only provide the central thrust with my own messages, but God has blessed us with the partnership of some of

America's finest leaders as different emphases have been made.

The ecclesiastical embrace of the Holy Spirit-begotten unity at our Pastors Seminar is observable by simply glancing over the following list. This multi-denominational list of gifted men who have accepted my invitation provides evidence that God is working to unite the hearts of spiritual leaders today. At least one common denominator of the following is that each man has addressed one conference in the last 10 years: Bill Bright, James Robison, Charles Blake, Luis Palau, Bill Hybels, Oral Roberts, Robert Schuller, Yonggi Cho, John MacArthur, Harold Brinkley, Gary Ezzo, James Dobson, John Maxwell, Billy Jo Daugherty, Jim Garlow, Charles Blair, Ed Silvoso, John Dawson, Peter Wagner, Ron Mehl, Ralph Moore, John Holland, Paul Walker, Glen Cole and Jim Cymbala are a wonderful sampling. Even as I write these words, I am anticipating this year's teammates: Bill McCartney, Rick Warren, Joe Garlington, James Ryle and Reinhard Bonnke.

God's smile *and direction* on our seminars has been a hallmark of divine grace, but at no time was His pleasure more manifest than in 1987 under the theme I had been moved to announce: "Taking Our Cities for God."

The rising political temperature, as candidates began sparing no preparation for the 1988 Presidential Election year, confirmed the appropriateness of our theme. It was the best of all times to be reminded and focused on what it does and does not mean when His people are called to "take" their cities for God. We had a uniquely timed opportunity to enunciate the true nature of the Church's call to pray for its nations and cities.

Perhaps few things are more difficult for some sincere saints to separate in their minds than the difference between political activism and aggressive intercession. While activists' political agendas are not necessarily opposed to spiritual objectives, the one *clear* assignment the people of God have been given is to intercede for their land and its leaders.

First Timothy 2:1-3 exhorts us all to prayer as our priority—"first of all"; that those in authority may be covered and supported by the prayers of the saints. Amazingly enough, the Holy Spirit's guidance in the Word does not suggest that supportive intercession is only to be made if we agree with the agenda or lifestyle of those holding the reigns of political power. Rather, He calls us to pray *for* leaders, and to war *against* evil powers in the invisible realm (see Eph. 6:10-12) so we can be a blessing to our culture. With this, He presents the promise of "peaceableness" in the society, but only *if the Church fulfills its intercessory role.* Further, the 1 Timothy text adds that this call is *very* pragmatic in God's purposes: He gives it for the high *purpose that a climate for evangelism may be created!* (see 1 Tim. 2:4,5).

In short, to "take a city for God," by the biblical definition, is not to gain control of city hall, but to break the dominion of oppressive spirits that obstruct the advance of God's Kingdom. His Kingdom, by Jesus' own definition, is transcendent of and separate from the transient and decaying structures of this world (see John 18:36). Its

TO "TAKE A CITY FOR GOD" IS TO WIN THE *HEARTS* OF THE PEOPLE OF A CITY TO KNOW THE LOVE OF CHRIST, NOT TO WIN ENOUGH POLITICAL POWER TO CONTROL THE GOVERNMENT.

advancement is the primary purpose of a praying people.

This priority, of course, does not disallow the propriety of believers in a free society seeking political roles or influence. It simply means that the purposes of the living Church are best served and least confused when these two agendas are spiritually discerned and clearly understood.

It *is* possible in a democratic society for committed believers to be employed in both—the spiritual mission of intercessory prayer, and a social mission of political activism. However, the objective of each must be kept in focus. To "take a city for God" is to win the *hearts* of the people of a city to know the love of Christ, not to win enough political power to control the government.

The 1987 seminar resonated with mighty confirmation of God's pleasure with our answer to a "citywide" vision for prayer. But now, the Lord was moving me further in follow-through to that first double-morning wake-up.

A THIRD STEP

About the same time I was preparing for that conference, the Holy Spirit illumined my heart to a third step in response to the call, *Pray against the destruction of your city.*

> # LOS ANGELES IS *NOT* A "MELTING POT." IT IS A MASSIVE MOSAIC OF SCORES OF SEPARATE CULTURES AND LINGUISTIC GROUPS, NOT AN AMALGAMATION. IT IS NOT SO MUCH THAT HOSTILITY DIVIDES THE CITY AS THAT DIVERSITY IS SO COMPLETELY PRESERVED BY SO MANY ETHNICITIES.

An unusual, throbbing constraint began to fill my heart. At first I felt highly reluctant, fearing that to answer this call might come off as casting myself in a role others would see as presumptuous, or self-important. But the prompting would not go away: *Gather pastors for citywide prayer.*

I became willing—but even then I knew the realities of "distance" and of factors that forged a gap between pastors in Los Angeles. At least three issues contribute to an obstacle of formidable proportions against realizing any unifying of our city's spiritual leadership:

1. Geographic distance.
First, Los Angeles County is one of the largest metropolitan areas in the world. The widespread nature of the city, joined to so regularly jammed traffic patterns, makes *any* invitation an object of serious analysis before anyone at anytime makes added commitments. I knew that busy pastors would be slow to consider driving dozens of miles on busy streets and clogged highways simply to attend "another meeting."
2. Cultural distance.
Second, Los Angeles is *not* a "melting pot." It is a massive

mosaic of scores of separate cultures and linguistic groups, not an amalgamation. It is not so much that hostility divides the city as that diversity is so completely preserved by so many ethnicities. The inevitable result is that inter-community communication—even among Christians—is very, very difficult. Cultural idiosyncrasies join to linguistic limitations to make efforts at homogenizing people an unparalleled challenge even among leaders in Christ's Body.

3. Denominational distance.

Finally, the historic lines of separatism that too frequently plague the Church and hinder its unity were no less present in our town. As a classical, pentecostal pastor with a known charismatic dimension to my ministry, I felt there was a very real limit to the circle of leaders who would even bother to answer a call or letter suggesting we get together. Compounding this was the ever-present potential sense of distrust that Christian leaders are vulnerable to feeling if a peer suggests a joint project: "What is he up to—really?"

None of these obstacles were observed either then or now in a spirit of cynicism. They simply represent a realism that needs to be and *can* be confronted and overcome. My challenge was in finding a way to start.

Our congregation had been given a beautiful house that overlooked the entirety of the San Fernando Valley—one of the major segments of the city of Los Angeles. The house sat almost astride a mountain that bridged to the basin—the downtown and coastal areas. We named it "The Hilltop" and this site became the temporary centerpiece for something wonderful God was about to do among a host of our city's spiritual leaders.

BEGINNINGS AT "THE HILLTOP"

For nearly a full year, I invited pastors to breakfast at "The Hilltop." The neutral setting seemed to help create a receptive mood toward meeting.

In extending my letter of invitation to meet together, I mentioned my desire to share simply with them—nearly a dozen at a time—

about something that had profoundly touched my heart regarding our city. My letter affirmed that I had no private agenda, no funds appeal to make, but only the desire to submit some thoughts for their judgment. I asked for an early hour (7:00 A.M., to beat the traffic!), and for approximately 100 minutes (for breakfast and interaction).

I contacted various leaders I knew and asked them to help me get names of men who represented different ethnic groups, different denominations and different parts of the city. It wasn't easy. The carved ruts of habit for us all left ridges that divided us—not so much in attitude as sheer visibility: we simply did not know each other was *there*.

My schedule could only handle about one breakfast every month, but during 1988 almost 100 pastors responded to my invitations. When each man at the table had shared the meal and some conversation that helped familiarize us with each other, I would then tell the story I used to begin this chapter: My call to "Pray against the destruction of the city of Los Angeles."

One of the most remarkable moments in my life (and memorable to all who were present that morning) occurred the instant I concluded my story with the first group during our breakfast together.

There was an earthquake!

It wasn't severe, but it was sharp enough to be disturbing; and it added a more than dramatic punctuation point to the content of my testimony.

We were all silent—waiting to discover the full magnitude of the tremor. Then, we were *moved*—all of us. It wasn't a matter of superstition, but it was with a joyful sense of conviction: God in His sovereign providence was calling us together. About this time, a beautiful partnership was bonded in the Spirit of God. To my view, it occurred at a double dimension.

THE INITIAL INVITATION FELLOWSHIP

First, Lloyd Ogilvie—then pastor of Hollywood's First Presbyterian Church, and now Chaplain of the United States Senate—became a private partner in my life personally, and in our group corporately. Lloyd and I had been friends for years, having met long before and having been teamed in a number of ways at city events since then. But the Holy Spirit seemed to be doing something unique in blending our hearts toward His purposes for Los Angeles's pastors.

Second, a smaller group within the more than one hundred who had breakfasted at one of the morning gatherings, began to meet for special times of brotherly comradeship and prayer. The group spanned a broad range of evangelicals, including pastors, denominational executives and parachurch leaders: Sonny Arguinzoni, Victory Outreach; Dennis Baker, Conservative Baptist Association; Charles Blake, West Angeles Church of God in Christ; Bill Brafford, Valley Community Church; Bill Burnett, Trinity Christian Center; Paul Cedar, Lake Avenue Congregational Church; Larry DeWitt, Calvary Community Church; Ray Diaz, Angelus Temple Hispanic Church; Dick Eastman, World Literature Crusade; Lee Eliason, Whittier Area Baptist Fellowship; Stephen Goold, Emmanuel Evangelical Free Church; Rosey Grier, "Are You Committed" Ministries; Paul Hackett, Crenshaw-Imperial Foursquare Church; Jack Hayford, The Church On The Way; Harold Helms, Angelus Temple; Bill Hoyt, Southwest Baptist Conference; Raimundo Jimenez, Hispanic Christian Communications Network; H. B. London, Jr., First Church of the Nazarene of Pasadena; Don Long, Southern California District, Foursquare; David Miller, Church at Rocky Peak; Roy McKeown, World Opportunities International; Donn Moomaw, Bel Air Presbyterian Church; Keith Phillips, World Impact; Ron Prinzing, Whittier First Assembly of God; Benjamin Reid, First Church of God; George Smith, North Hollywood Assembly of God; Wilbur Wacker, Calvary Church of the Coastlands.

It was one morning while most of this group were literally "on our faces"—prostrate in prayer and humility, scattered across the huge carpeted area in The Hilltop's living room—that a conviction was born. We believed we were to call the pastors of our city together—whoever would come. But because no precedent to this had been establised in more than a quarter century, we had no idea if we would be there alone—just over a score of us—or if others would come.

But we knew God wanted to do something more. It was clear to us that a special sense of brotherhood occurred when we prayed together. We wanted to share this with other pastors. And we hadn't forgotten: God wanted *prayer* to go forth—to save our city from destruction. He wanted us as sheperds to love our city into the Kingdom.

2

PRAY TOGETHER

OUT OF THE BASEMENT, INTO THE STREETS

BY TED HAGGARD

"Police! Everyone against the wall with your hands up!" someone shouted as a door flew open with a bang.

My body fearfully jerked awake in the dark room of the Uptown Hotel in south-central Colorado Springs. In the darkness, I groped for my glasses so I could read the digital clock beaming 1:04 A.M. Trying to remember where I was, I could see police lights flashing on my window and hear people in another room sobbing while others shouted and swore.

I just wanted to pray over this section of the city for three days. I didn't plan on being in the middle of a violent drug bust! I eased out of bed and cautiously looked out the window to see eight police cars blazing their headlights at room 137. The noise and shouting created a sense of chaos. I didn't want to be noticed looking out the window for fear of being shot. I discreetly watched as police cars quickly came and went. The police searched and confiscated some items from both the targeted room and a car parked just outside. They handcuffed two men, while a woman stood crying in the doorway as they left.

I'm getting out of here right now, I thought to myself. As I turned to my still dark and now eerie motel room, I realized I was safer locked in my room than I would be if I tried to walk to my car and leave. I was trapped.

I quietly rechecked the flimsy chain on my door and slowly climbed back into bed. Listening carefully, I could hear a child crying, a woman cussing and the muffled murmuring of a couple in the next room. Four men stood outside my room about 15 feet from my door talking and drinking. I felt confused, vulnerable and foolish. The men outside scared me, but the sound of police cars patrolling nearby somehow brought comfort. I drifted off to sleep thinking of my wife and children safe in their beds on the other side of the city.

Screaming and the sound of shattering glass jolted me awake again in what seemed like only moments later. In the daze of deep sleep, I found myself reaching for my glasses through the darkness. I lunged toward the window and glanced at the clock—3:07 A.M. A woman was screaming and people were running toward her. She had just thrown a chair through the plate-glass window of her motel room. After a few minutes, I heard police sirens approaching—the sound made her increasingly distraught. She, too, was arrested that night as I watched from my room, praying for my city.

The next morning I saw this section of the city from a new perspective. In the morning light, it felt once again like the resort city of Colorado Springs. The sky was bright blue with its beautiful white, fluffy clouds. Birds were singing and the grass looked green and well kept. The air was crisp and refreshing. Well-dressed, health-conscious people were going about their business, laughing and enjoying one another. Everything was peaceful. And the only evidence that anything unusual had happened the night before was the one broken window casually being cleaned up by a janitor. But to me the city looked and felt different...very different.

Mark Marble, an associate pastor from our church, met me that morning and we began to walk through the streets praying as we went.

We were motivated to pray because we knew God wanted to

establish significant ministries in the area. Years earlier, the Lord had impressed upon us His vision for our city, but incidents from the previous night demonstrated that God's will was far from the present reality. People here were in trouble.

Soon after our prayerwalk, a life-giving church relocated to this area from the suburbs and began intense local ministry. In addition, Nicky Cruz and others launched effective outreach ministries in this troubled section of our city. Not only have Christian ministries been working there, but social agencies and community groups have also launched efforts in the area to serve people. I wouldn't claim that our prayers exclusively caused these positive developments to take place, but I do believe they hindered some potentially negative developments and opened the door for greater spiritual light.

PRAYER: SEEING WHAT GOD SEES

Several years ago, Danny Ost, a missionary from Mexico City, said that when we pray God gives us:

- Jesus pacemakers so our hearts will be moved by the things that move the heart of God;
- Jesus contact lenses so we can see people the way He sees them;
- Jesus hearing aides so our ears will be able to clearly hear His voice and the voices of the "crying, sighing and dying."

Ost understood that as God touches our hearts, He changes what we see and hear. He also emphasized that through prayer God gives us the strength to effectively go to and touch people. Jesus shoes and Jesus gloves become a part of our lives only through prayer.

I experienced God's transforming power through prayer in a vivid way in 1984. My wife, Gayle, and I were on vacation in Colorado Springs to visit her family. At that time we were serving at Bethany World Prayer Center just outside Baton Rouge, Louisiana. We were very happy and thought we would probably serve there the rest of our lives.

Colorado Springs, in contrast, seemed eerie. Christian pastors and friends told Gayle and me how it had gained a reputation as a pastors' graveyard. They told us about churches struggling and Satanic activity and witchcraft occurring in nearby Manitou Springs. Even though the city was beautiful, it was not known as an attractive place for Christians. These negative reports caused me to hold a dismal view of the spiritual climate in Colorado Springs.

While on vacation, Gayle wanted some time with her family and I wanted to spend some time in the nearby Rocky Mountains. So I took a pup tent into the forest west of Pikes Peak for three days of prayer and fasting.

During that time the Lord changed my view of Colorado Springs. He did exactly what Ost taught:

- He placed a Jesus pacemaker in my heart. Suddenly I became confident that the gospel had a bright future in Colorado Springs.
- He placed Jesus contact lenses in my eyes. Immediately I saw the city according to His plan. The reality of what was had been transcended by what could and would be if His people would only pray and believe.
- He placed Jesus hearing aids in my ears. I began to hear things differently—not only about the lost, but also about the churches in the city.

A new voice seemed to be speaking. It was as if I could hear the heart of God. Colorado Springs was no longer dismal and dark, but beautiful and bright. The reports that had formerly caused me to feel discouraged now gave rise to a sense of anticipation in me as I recognized the great opportunities that accompanied them. I received supernatural hope.

PRAYER: TUNING IN TO GOD'S HEART

God began dropping ideas into my heart about specific ways to touch people. He was calling me to Colorado Springs. He spoke to me about things that needed to be done, and how He would bring the correct combination of people into the city so His plan could be fulfilled. *For three days God let me see His plan.* It was a new picture accompanied with a flood of ideas.

In the midst of divine revelation, He communicated clearly that His plan could not be achieved by one man—not even by one ministry. His corporate Body would need to function in harmony to accomplish His task. He was calling me to be a catalyst. God wanted His Body in Colorado Springs to impact the city.

As I prayed, I remembered that T.L. Osborn, another great missionary, said that the primary way God gives His children their daily bread is by giving them new ideas. The Holy Spirit was pregnant with vision for Colorado Springs. He had the plans, the pictures, the concepts...the future. They came so fast....It felt as though His ideas had been anxiously awaiting a listener.

I believe what happened to me near Pikes Peak was the direct result of the many faithful believers in Colorado Springs who had been praying and serving patiently for years. The believers at the Navigators, Christian Booksellers Association, Compassion International as well as those in healthy local churches, such as First Presbyterian, St. John's Baptist and Agape Fellowship, had been praying for spiritual renewal in our city.

Now several years have passed. Although our city still has a long way to go, we are experiencing substantial conversion growth in many churches. Parachurch ministries (servant ministries) are continuing to move into our city; negative social trends are being addressed in positive ways; and a large network of churches called "The Net" coordinates prayer, evangelism and service projects throughout our community.

PRAYER AND FASTING: THE POTENT COMBINATION

I now know what I had only suspected at the time: It was prayer and fasting that opened my ears to hear what the Holy Spirit was saying. God forcefully impacts our lives when we open ourselves through prayer and fasting, even though we don't consciously realize it is happening. It causes us to line up with God's purpose, which is for the Body of Christ to make it hard to go to hell from our cities. Without His purpose, our efforts easily degenerate into impotent attempts to "do the right thing."

Prayer and fasting not only changed my view of Colorado Springs, allowing the Holy Spirit to infuse me with His ideas, but it also gave me greater confidence, an understanding of spiritual authority and a renewed revelation of His Word. The following three

IT'S THE SPIRIT OF GOD THAT MAKES THE BIBLE MEANINGFUL, AND IT'S THE BIBLE THAT MAKES THE SPIRIT UNDERSTANDABLE.

ideas were the concepts I needed to understand in order for our city-wide efforts to be effective.

1. *Humble confidence.* Working in harmony with one another can only be achieved as we create a balance between the confidence we have in our roles within the city and humility. The humility gained through prayer and fasting makes it possible for us to willingly serve and strengthen one another.

One of my first assignments from the Lord in Colorado Springs was to submit to the spiritual authority of a key pastor there. Some have said that the network of churches in Colorado Springs functions well because the major churches and servant-ministry leaders are comfortable with one another. We have found that the necessary trust enabling us to serve each other is appropriated through extended times with God. Therefore I'm convinced that a lifestyle of prayer and fasting is irreplaceable in developing the confidence and humility necessary to be effective.

2. *Increased spiritual authority.* For too many years Christians have suffered under the misdirection of well-meaning spiritual leaders who lack both the anointing of the Holy Spirit on their work and the spiritual power to birth and maintain genuine ministry. Both Watchman Nee's book *Spiritual Authority* and Gene Edwards's *Tale of Three Kings* are excellent books that teach us some of the mysteries about spiritual authority.

I tell my staff members that it is a miracle of God when anyone comes to church. It is a gift from God when we are able to speak meaningfully into another person's heart, and it requires much more than our own thoughts and plans to bring effective harmony to the Body of Christ.

Mediocre times of prayer together are at best worthless, maybe even detrimental. They appease our thirst for genuine spirituality and sometimes keep us from achieving authentic spiritual break-through for our cities. But through earnest, engaging prayer and fasting, God breathes into His people a spiritual dynamic that produces life, freedom, inspiration, power and purpose in our efforts, causing them to be successful—by eternal standards.

3. *Heightened revelation.* Prayer and fasting infuses the Word of God into our hearts. It's the Spirit of God that makes the Bible mean-ingful, and it's the Bible that makes the Spirit understandable. After praying and fasting, my Bible-reading life is remarkably fresh again. I have come to believe that prayer and fasting is the primary way to

Do not watch television while you fast. Try to limit your sensory input to pure things.

move us out of the desert and into the fresh streams of His life. In that flow, His plans and purposes become clear.

Not only does prayer and fasting increase the force of the Word in us, but it also helps us receive and grow in His gifts. After prayer and fasting, I find myself operating more naturally in the fruit of the Spirit. Greater revelation of the spiritual dynamics in myself, my family, my church and my city are heightened when I submit to this spiritual discipline.

God has been emphasizing the importance of prayer and fasting to His Body in the last few years through books such as Dr. Bill Bright's *The Coming Revival, America's Call to Fast, Pray, and Seek God's Face* and Elmer Towns's *Fasting for Spiritual Breakthrough, A Guide to Nine Biblical Fasts.* Interest is so high in the Body of Christ, even the old classics are surfacing again: *Your Appointment with God, A Bible Study on Fasting* by Gwen Shaw and *God's Chosen Fast* by Arthur Wallis.

OK, How Do You Do It!?

It's simple! Just take along a Bible, Scripture audiocassettes and a tape player, a trustworthy book and some water or juice. Go to a place where you can walk around and pray—maybe a rural camp for solitude, or a downtown area where you can prayerwalk. If you want to prayerwalk in the city, have a good friend join you while prayerwalking, or people will think you are mumbling to yourself (which might open the door for an adventurous ministry to nice people who wear white coats to work).

Do not watch television while you fast. Try to limit your sensory input to pure things. You are going to hate it. (Smile!) You will be bored, you will run out of things to pray about, and, if you are secluded, you will be convinced that the president of the United States is trying to call you. While praying and fasting, you will be tempted to do things you despise, and you will create enough projects to last 10 lifetimes.

As you sense your body starting to resent you, you will actually see fried chicken, mashed potatoes and gravy, green beans, corn, Big Macs, French fries and nachos strewn across the sky when you glance up in prayer, or manifesting in the print of the wallpaper when you lie in your room at night. I usually crave Cashew nuts! You know you've really lost it when you start looking up Scriptures that refer to "honey" or "cream" so you can "meditate on the Word." At these times I remind myself that I am more hungry for God than for these things—God likes that.

After your fast, you will discover that God has filled your spiritual motor with jet fuel. You will be refreshed in the Scriptures, renewed in His Spirit and refocused on your purpose and direction. The new vision Ost spoke of and the innovative ideas Osborn suggested will fill you. A revelation of His Body—the fact that one brother, sister or ministry can't fulfill His purpose without the other—beckons loudly after praying and fasting.

Oh, one other note: While praying and fasting, rest and listen to Scripture tapes as much as possible. Your body needs the rest and your spirit will love what I call "soaking in the Word."

These times of personal prayer will give God the opportunity to settle the vast majority of the issues that destroy most ministries. The fear of failure, rejection, pride, lust, arrogance, self-centeredness, time management issues and financial confusion can all be dealt with in an atmosphere of prayer and fasting. As we grow in ministry, we have a choice: Either we allow God to work out issues privately through prayer and fasting, or we will force God to take care of those issues publicly. It's our choice. (I choose prayer and fasting!)

PRAYER: TOGETHER WE STAND

During the last few years, we have seen several ministries emphasize the necessity of cross-denominational prayer. David Bryant's Concerts of Prayer, Joe Aldrich's Prayer Summits, Dick Eastman's Schools of Prayer, Bill Bright's Prayer and Fasting emphasis and Paul Cedar's Mission America are all, along with many others, working to facilitate broad-based city and regionwide prayer efforts.

Books such as Steve Hawthorn's *Prayerwalking* and my book, *Primary Purpose*, are being used with Ed Silvoso's *That None Should Perish* and John Dawson's set of books *Taking Our Cities for God* and *Healing America's Wounds*. Peter Wagner's excellent six-volume prayer series has given us the information needed to pray effectively in various formats. These and many other excellent books provide specific direction for those who want to make the significant impact upon their cities that can only be birthed through prayer. The emphasis on broad-based prayer is being embraced throughout the Christian world. For example:

- In 1993, the United Prayer Track of the A.D. 2000 Movement, led by Peter Wagner, coordinated an effort that networked 21,879,000 Christians from 105 countries worldwide to pray for the evangelization of the 10/40 window.
- In 1995, the same group coordinated 36,700,000 intercessors from 101 nations to pray for the evangelization of the lost in the 100 gateway cities of the 10/40 window.
- In 1997, millions of Christians will unite in prayer for the 1,739 remaining unreached people groups.
- While this book is being written, plans are under way

to construct a "World Prayer Center" in Colorado
Springs that will serve as a state-of-the-art information
collection and dissemination hub serving prayer ministries throughout the world.

These efforts include Christians from every major Christian tradition. They speak different languages, dress differently and worship
differently. They are from divergent cultures and embrace a wide variety of traditions. But they all believe in the Lordship of Jesus Christ
and the authority of the Bible. They actually do pray in harmony.

Why, though, is this happening on such a massive scale for the
first time in the history of the Church? Why is the Lord demanding
that His people unite with others in prayer?

BROAD-BASED PRAYER, AN UNSTOPPABLE EVANGELISTIC FORCE

When praying with believers from differing traditions, God's vision
in us is strengthened by the Body's diversity. From those relationships and from the prayer itself, God forms an unstoppable evangelistic force. For example, in today's (August 23, 1996) Colorado
Springs newspaper, *The Gazette Telegraph* ran four major articles about
Christian activities:

- On the front page is an article featuring Nicky Cruz's
  outreach effort to gangs and those affected by "the
  streets." The result was 13,000 gang and gang-related
  people hearing the gospel;
- Another front-page article describes church leaders
  uniting with city officials to prevent the arson problems that have occurred in Southern churches from
  developing in Colorado Springs;
- On the front page of Section B is a story about a picnic
  for the homeless hosted by the Salvation Army and
  The Net (network of churches). The article is accompanied by a picture of a believer sharing Christ with a
  homeless person;
- Another article on the front of Section B is about

Reverend Lee's efforts to organize and unite the citizens of the Hillside community (an area we prayer-walked in the opening story of this chapter), which has resulted in lower crime and gang problems. The article focused on the improvements that have been made in the community as a result of this labor of love.

Obviously, we don't experience positive news like this every day in our city. But these stories clearly remind us that the eyes of the secular press do notice when the diverse Body is ministering to people in ways that create authentic change.

Paul's discussions in 1 Corinthians 12 about the strength of the diverse Body and the necessity of our serving one another become actualized in our lives when we are praying with a believer from another Christian tradition. We in God's Body need to be molded together through united prayer, praying as one body. Then, the new visions and ideas He has planted in individual members can be refined so they can become a reality through the strength of His Body—our combined strength.

One afternoon last summer (1995), I was feeling alone and inadequate as I drove to the pastors' prayer meeting at Christ Community Church. An elder who had been with our congregation for 10 years had just left our church. On his way out he told me that I was not an adequate Bible teacher (which, incidentally, is true, but I just hate it when people tell me what I already know!). He also said, "Evangelism isn't everything."

So as I drove to the meeting, I was experiencing feelings of pity, loneliness, inadequacy and a gut-wrenching suspicion that New Life Church was going to collapse because of me. I walked into the prayer meeting and saw several pastors singing, reading Scripture and praying. Steve Todd, the president of our local Association of Evangelicals, placed a chair in the middle of the circle and asked anyone who needed prayer to sit in the chair.

I eased into the chair and told them that I was feeling pretty low, and that although the criticism this elder was leveling against me might be true, it still saddened me. My heart felt empty. I explained that I had prayed alone as much as I could about this situation, but I needed their prayers and friendship.

The pastors gathered around me to pray. Before they began, however, one pastor spoke up and said:

> Pastor Ted, I have something to confess. I have had a secret desire in my heart that you would make a serious mistake so your church would get into trouble. I knew if large numbers of people left your church, then my church would pick up maybe a hundred of them, which would double my size. Brother, I repent for that attitude, and I promise to start praying privately and publicly for God to bless you and cause New Life to grow even more.

Boy did that cheer me up!

Just about the time I thought I couldn't possibly get any lower, another brother spoke up:

> Ted, I have something to say, too. I've had some of my members leave my church to start attending your church. When that happened, it made me feel angry and bitter toward them and you. They said they wanted to go to New Life because of the youth program, but I knew they just didn't like our church as much as they liked yours. Because of that, even though I've been cordial toward you, I haven't liked what you are doing. I really wanted you to fail. I felt good when I heard something bad about you or New Life. I'm sorry. Today I realize that we're all just men trying to serve Him. I want to be a blessing to you, brother.

I had asked the very guys to pray for me that had secretly been hoping for my demise.

As the prayer began, however, it was clear that in asking these men to pray for me, the Lord had done a miracle in both my heart and theirs. We became more than pastors working in the same city; we became sincere friends. Our hearts were changed in that setting saturated in humility and confession so we could effectively collaborate together in Him.

Since that time, the security and strength of our relationships have opened the door to not only my own rekindled conviction about my leadership at New Life, but also to a strengthened conviction for all the pastors who prayed together that day. We are now a stronger

WE NO LONGER COMPETE...
WE COMPLETE HIS BODY.

team for God to use. We no longer compete...we complete His Body. As a group we had to resolve the issues in His presence, which made us into a stronger team. Thus, it is harder to go to hell from our community.

Without the security of broad-based relationships built through united and supportive prayer, Nicky Cruz could never have spoken to 13,000 kids in our city auditorium with the communitywide support of the local churches. Nor would there be support for Reverend Lee's community activities. The Salvation Army and The Net wouldn't have been willing to cooperate, and we wouldn't have the relationships to prevent the threat of arson.

I'm not saying that all of these ministries, and others, are a direct result of prayer meetings the leaders of these particular ministries have attended. I do believe, however, that when leaders pray together, a spiritual climate is established that promotes increased effectiveness and greater grace for believers' efforts. In this kind of atmosphere, even the secular community increases in its wisdom with effectiveness.

We are either successful together through the bond of prayer, or we begin to fragment from each another and die in our ineffectiveness. Just as the members of our natural bodies are interdependent, so the Body of Christ is interdependent.

INTERDEPENDENCE, THE STRENGTH OF HIS BODY

We were pleased after the Promise Keepers pastors' meeting in Atlanta. Why? Because 10 percent of the evangelical pastors in America joined together and blessed one another. As they worshiped, prayed and learned together, they discovered they were a team that could accomplish their purpose by utilizing their combined strength. The conference strengthened thousands of churches by giving pastors an opportunity to grow together.

We know how to be successful independently. Now God is teaching us how to be more successful, with greater ease, by becoming interdependent. We Christians can only be successful, to a point, independent of others. But to grow to maturity, we must interact with a diverse body of believers. We need to learn from and grow with them. That's why we have families and communities. And that's why God is now calling groups of local churches together in our cities to form families and become interdependent. We have a purpose, and that purpose is best fulfilled in a group. We are most effective that way.

When God directed Joe Aldrich of Multnomah College to start encouraging groups of pastors to come together to pray for each other, the idea caught on like wildfire. At a Prayer Summit pastors have adequate time for God to build them into a team. Thus, a solid body of trusting pastors is formed that can effectively network to promote the gospel with greater harmony in the community.

When pastors pray together and become interdependent they:

- Develop friendships and bonds of trust;
- Establish a foundation for partnerships;
- Enjoy greater effectiveness in promoting the gospel;
- Lead with ease and assurance.

The Body is edified when Christian leaders are at liberty to publicly bless each other or include one another in illustrations that demonstrate respect and friendship. We have developed an effective Bodybuilding exercise! We copy lists of churches from the Yellow Pages, distributing them to our parishioners so they can pray for them. This builds character in our church body and unity in His corporate Body. Any edifying group prayer efforts, if done in humility and with servants' hearts, will build a spiritual army that the enemy cannot overcome.

Thus, it becomes easy to coordinate a multichurch effort to prayer-walk an entire city. Utilizing the strength of an interdependent Body of believers makes it possible to pray for every person, business, school and government building. Last September (1995), 130 churches in Colorado Springs united to host a Harvest Crusade with Greg Laurie. In preparation for that event, we worked together to prayer-walk our city four and a half times. That united prayer effort allowed us to function in a practical way as a true Body.

We have sponsored pastors' prayer and fasting retreats, pastors' Prayer Summits and regionwide Concerts of Prayer. Many groups of pastors meet regularly in the city to pray together. Periodically, The Net or our local Association of Evangelicals will call us together for times of extended prayer, or prayer and fasting. When we do this for extended time periods, we always notice a change in how we see people, respond to people, hear people, touch people and go to people. It makes our jobs easier. It creates an atmosphere of interdependence in our Christian community. And in that atmosphere it is easy to implement His plan. We can do it as a Body...that prays together.

RESULT: AN INCREASED CORPORATE WITNESS

When our country was dominated by a Judeo-Christian culture, we could measure our effectiveness by the strength of our church budgets, the number of those in our Sunday School and church attendance, or the size of our worship facilities. Now, though, we are looking for measurement systems that more accurately gauge our effectiveness in the community.

Formerly, we may have had the following goals:

- We want our budget and attendance to increase 10 percent this year.
- We need to build a new youth facility to attract more families.

Now, however, we must also add to those objectives targets such as the following:

- We must pray for every person in the city at least once a year.
- We must communicate the gospel, in an understandable way, to every person in our vicinity at least once a year.

- We must raise the percentage of people attending life-giving churches in our city by 1 percent a year.

We can achieve the first set of objectives by strengthening our own local churches through simple transfer growth, convincing people that our church is better than the one they used to attend. Consequently, if we evaluate our effectiveness using the first set of objectives, we might deceive ourselves. We may have a growing church that gives us the illusion that we are changing our city, but in reality we are not having any measurable impact. Thus, we have growing churches in the midst of a spiritually declining culture.

But the second set of objectives demands that we work together to actually make a measurable difference in our cities. If our measurement system is based upon the percentage of people attending life-giving churches on an average Sunday morning, then one or two churches doing a great job is no longer sufficient. We need dozens, if not hundreds of churches growing simultaneously through conversion growth to see overall, citywide penetration of the gospel message.

How can we do it? By utilizing the strength of the whole Body. By moving in unity. By paying the price in private prayer and fasting to gain His vision, combined with corporate prayer to utilize the strength of His Body.

We can get healthy together!

And what will be the result? An increased corporate witness that easily produces growth.

RESOURCES FOR
"PRAYING TOGETHER"

CREATING SPIRITUAL UNITY TO FULFILL A
SPIRITUAL MISSION

CONTRIBUTORS:
JOE ALDRICH
DAVID BRYANT
BILL BRIGHT
C. PETER WAGNER
ED SILVOSO
STEVE HAWTHORNE

This chapter is a menu of resources for the development of prayer in your community. In chapter two I [Ted Haggard] emphasized the importance of praying together to make it harder to go to hell from our cities. In this chapter, six outstanding prayer leaders introduce helpful ideas and resources explaining *how to* pray and build a city-wide prayer base. As you read these articles, you may find approaches to implement in your city now. Others may require a year or two before your city is ready for them. Through prayer the Holy Spirit will guide and instruct you.

THE MEANING AND PURPOSE OF A PRAYER SUMMIT

BY JOE ALDRICH

JOE ALDRICH

Dr. Joseph Aldrich is president of Multnomah Bible College and Biblical Seminary and its ministries. He also serves on the faculty in the Doctor of Ministry programs for Dallas and Talbot seminaries. Dr. Aldrich is a faculty member of Billy Graham Schools of Evangelism. He has enriched God's kingdom through his national radio and television broadcasts; international conferences; and note-worthy publications, which include his best-selling books *Lifestyle Evangelism* and *Reunitus*.

I define a Prayer Summit as:

A four-day worship experience attended by a diversity of Christian leaders from specific communities, whose singular purpose is to seek God, His kingdom and His righteousness. The expectation is that He will guide them through a humbling, healing, uniting process that will lead them to a unity of heart, mind and mission, and will qualify them for the blessing of God.

The Acts 2 church had a unity of heart, mind and mission, and God added daily to their number those who were being saved. Unity created a setting that allowed large numbers of people to be saved. So the bottom-line questions that face Christian leaders are:

1. What would it take to initiate and sustain a work of God in a specific geographical community? And,
2. What would it take to see John 17 lived out in answer to the Son's prayer?

UNITY, THE HIGHEST FORM OF EVANGELISM

Satan split the angelic ranks, the first family, the Davidic Kingdom and has, quite successfully, split the Church. Three times Jesus asked His Father to protect believers and make them one "as we are one." The Trinity is the model for unity. They function together in full support of each other. There is unanimity in all they do, say and think; yet each retains His integrity as a functioning being.

The Lord prays (see John 17) that the world (18 times) and God's glory (9 times) will somehow get together so the world will know that God sent Christ, and will know that God loves them. If they understand Christ's divine origin and the Father's love, they are not far from the cross! It should not surprise us that unity is the highest form of evangelism. Its message is revolutionary. At the core of the universe exists a triune God who dwells together in unity. If only a shattered, broken, divided world could catch a whiff of unity!

Meanwhile, churches split, divisions reign, pastors experience moral failure, homes fall apart and dreams are shattered. God's plan is to allow His reborn children to be the vehicle through which He reveals His existence in complete unity. We are inducted into the family of God as members of the second incarnation, called to make visible the invisible God. How? Unity!

"How good and pleasant it is when brothers dwell together in unity...there the Lord bestows his blessing" (Ps. 133: 1,3).

- So how do you get Kingdom-building, denomination-
ally-bound, doctrinally-separated leaders to recognize
that in every city, there is only one Church and many
congregations?
- How will they overcome the pride that precludes
God's blessings?
- What would unity look like in a larger community of
faith?

I thought of bringing in some ecclesiastical heavyweights and
turning them loose on the pastors in a given area. You and I know it
wouldn't work. God always resists the proud, but gives grace
(enablement) to the humble. He exalts them at the proper time. That's
it. Pride and humility are antithetical. There will be no unity without
humility. Repentance and reconciliation are the kinds of things experienced when genuine humility is reached.

TRANSFORMED IN THE PRESENCE OF THE KING

What is needed is an environment where leaders feel safe and can
leave behind their differences and be surprised by their commonali-
ties. I concluded we were looking at three or four days in His presence to bring us to a point of brokenness and humility. We can't
preach them into it, lectures wouldn't help. Leaders need to spend
four days with the King.

And then it hit me. The key to coming to a point of humility, of
confession for sin and of deliverance from sin is to spend prolonged time in His presence worshiping the King with no other
agenda: No church business allowed. No one in charge except the
Holy Spirit. Generally, no prayers for "problems back home." Hour
after hour we worship. We sing over 100 songs a day. Scripture is
read, prayers are spontaneously given. Often the presence of the
Lord is so strong we don't dare speak. It's holy ground. Men lie on
the carpet prostrate before the King. Tears flow as God begins the
breaking process. The following is the process. It has at least five
parts:

His Holiness> Humility> Unity> Community> Impact

To impact our cities, we must understand that:

- There will be no *impact* without a healthy *community* of faith. If we want a citywide revival, we need a citywide church.
- There will be no *community* without *unity*. A house or church divided against itself will not stand.
- There will be no *unity* without *humility*. This is where repentance and reconciliation unusually take place. Can you imagine pastors asking forgiveness from fellow pastors in the community? It happens at every Prayer Summit.
- There will be no *humility* apart from encountering *His holiness*. Like Isaiah, we cry out, "Woe is me! for I am undone; because I am a man of unclean lips, and I dwell in the midst of a people of unclean lips: for mine eyes have seen the King, the Lord of hosts" (Isa. 6:5, *KJV*).

So how does this all work?

After hours of praise, worship and adoration, the "hated chair" is put in the center of the circle. Leaders empty their hearts. It all comes pouring out. The hurts and pains, the logjams of the past are broken up. Deliverance from satanic bondage is not an unusual experience. As the dam bursts, the wounded warrior is surrounded by men who place their hands upon him and lift him into the presence of the Great Physician.

MELTING HEARTS TOGETHER

Leaders are invited to share whatever is keeping them in bondage. Unfinished business with parents, families and peers is settled. Some are hooked on pornography, others have been forgiven, but not delivered from some pattern of sin. Satan uses this sin from their past to discourage them and keep them in bondage. Asking men to pray for God's deliverance and then to experience freedom melts hearts together as we share our common humanity. The changes in their countenances are obvious. These men, in a matter of hours, become best friends. They attest to the fact that their Prayer Summit was the highlight of their walk with the Lord. In 95 percent of the cases, they continue to meet weekly when they return home.

Significant, vital, lasting change takes place. Denominational barriers come down. Caricatures are eliminated. Relationships are developed. Joint services are planned for the future. Covenants are often made, enabling them to truly become the Church of their communities. Pulpits are exchanged, dates are compared, schedules are coordinated. Many meet weekly, and then take a full day once a month for praise and worship. They do not want their new prayer times to resemble lifeless ministerial meetings. They now want to come together to worship and pray. They become best friends and co-laborers.

I actually discovered some of these dynamics when I pastored, and wondered what it would take to make and maintain unity. Two days on a mountainside with the elders knit us together. I believe the time we spent there was the major cause of very rapid growth.

In some communities, four or five pastors and their elders are getting away to meet with the King. Their approaches to worship change. They become hooked on singing without accompaniment. Nothing is as beautiful as the voices of people whose souls are being restored by the Good Shepherd.

Weekend Prayer Summits for the men of a church have proven to be most successful. I guess we should not be surprised that time in His presence changes lives, realigns ministries and saves marriages.

For further instruction, my book *Reunitus* is available in most Christian bookstores. Around the world, the results in the presence of the King are the same.

To receive more information about Prayer Summits, contact:

Dr. Joe Aldrich
Multnomah Bible College and Biblical Seminary
8435 NE Gilsan
Portland, OR 97220
Phone: (503) 255-0332

CONCERTS OF PRAYER

BY DAVID BRYANT

DAVID BRYANT

David Bryant is founder and president of Concerts of Prayer International, and Chairman of America's National Prayer Committee. He and his team have conducted hundreds of citywide mass prayer rallies for renewal and evangelism; trained tens of thousands of pastors to focus their congregations on spiritual awakening; and networked national leaders and ministries into coalitions that promote revival. He hosts a daily radio program, and shares in the leadership of international efforts for world evangelization. His training materials as well as his latest book *THE HOPE AT HAND: National and World Revival for the 21st Century* (Baker) have received wide acclaim.

It is clear from both Scripture and the history of the Church: God moves in amazing ways when people are praying in unison.

Right now, many nations are witnessing the dramatic growth of grassroots movements of united prayer.

Like feeder streams, these movements of prayer are rising and expanding. It is our firm conviction they will soon build and converge into a literal torrent of focused united prayer, carrying the Church into a time of dramatic spiritual renewal.

We will then see a time of sweeping moral and spiritual rebirth in North America and beyond, fueling a global thrust toward worldwide evangelization.

The Concerts of Prayer movement is helping to dig trenches between these prayer movements, directing all the divergent streams of prayer and revival together into what we believe will become a raging river of genuine, widespread spiritual awakening to Jesus Christ. Already hundreds of cities, thousands of churches and hundreds of thousands of Christians have joined in Concerts of Prayer throughout the past 10 years.

PROMOTING A UNITED VISION

The term "concerts of prayer" actually dates back to the great spiritual awakening of the early 1700s. At that time puritan Jonathan Edwards called for concerts of prayer to promote a united vision in prayer among God's people. The purpose for those prayers? Spiritual revival and the advancement of God's kingdom on earth.

Helping to promote this same united vision of prayer for our generation, a Concert of Prayer is vitally important to the prayer movement as a whole.

One distinctive of a Concert of Prayer is that it gathers a broad representation of pray-ers. In a citywide Concert of Prayer, Christians unite across various boundaries: denominational, institutional, min-

UNITED PRAYER IS KEY TO ANY SPIRITUAL REVIVAL.

isterial, social, generational, ethnic, cultural and even across minor doctrinal boundaries.

Additionally, the whole Body of Christ in a community or church meets around the larger biblical concerns for spiritual awakening and world evangelization.

Like a grand symphony, pray-ers blend their hearts, minds and voices by faith in God's Word. Basing the prayer agenda upon Scripture, they intercede harmoniously with one another and with all God has promised for His Church and for His world.

Participants in a Concert of Prayer submit to the Holy Spirit, who "orchestrates" each prayer meeting so one prayer theme builds upon another according to the will of God. In fact, we could say that Jesus Himself is the "concert master" who leads the "composition" of intercession in His name, which the Father delights to both hear and answer abundantly.

MORE THAN AN EVENT—IT'S A MOVEMENT

Concerts of Prayer International (COPI) was founded in 1988, and built on a dream for what God might do in our nation and our world through a widespread spiritual awakening to Christ.

United prayer is key to any spiritual revival. Therefore, the organization was dedicated to serving the Church by promoting, equipping and mobilizing movements of united prayer that seek God for spiritual awakening and worldwide evangelization.

A Concert of Prayer is much more than a one-night event. It is part of a growing cycle of prayer within a community or city. Eventually it will build and join with prayer movements in other cities, culminating in God's answer to our prayers—a global, spiritual awakening to Christ.

In fact, the Concerts of Prayer movement encompasses a broad range of outreach efforts as it:

1. *Presents the "Message of Hope"—igniting and sustaining an expectation for the coming spiritual awakening to Christ.* COPI currently teams with organizations such as Promise Keepers to present the message of hope to large gatherings of pastors; preaches the message of hope at other large assemblies of pastors, leaders and Christian students; produces materials that inspire believers to join the united prayer movement; and organizes and leads mass rallies and strategic Concerts of Prayer at locations throughout the world.

2. *Ministers to local pastors and churches, working to unite the Body of Christ across ethnic, racial and denominational lines.* In Metro New York, COPI's Urban Strategy division is modeling and serving urban prayer movements by directing urban consultations for prayer leaders; organizing dozens of Concerts of Prayer events; gathering pas-

tors, laymen and missionaries from different ethnic backgrounds around a Metropolitan Prayer Covenant calling for revival, reconciliation, reformation and reaching the lost; administrating The Lord's Watch (an ongoing 24-hour-a-day prayer vigil with thousands of participants in more than 100 churches); and hosting Pastors' Prayer Summits, Unity Dinners and regional leaders' meetings.

3. *Provides tools for prayer leaders.* The COPI Services division creates many training tools for pastors and church leaders related to spiritual awakening, prayer and prayer events—including how-to training materials for leading a Concert of Prayer, vision-casting videos about the movement of united prayer toward revival, as well as many other pamphlets, books and cassettes.

4. *Networks among national Christian leaders to present a united vision for revival to the entire Church.* For example, COPI currently provides leadership within American's National Prayer Committee; facilitates events related to the National Day of Prayer in May and the National Concert of Prayer in October; fosters communication among local prayer movements; and consults with national outreach leaders to clarify the united vision for revival throughout the Church.

5. *Links individual believers in united prayer.* COPI produces the daily two-minute National Concert of Prayer radio feature, which both models and actually unites listeners in prayer. It also distributes a quarterly publication that provides news of local, national and international prayer movements.

6. *Influences the global Christian community in concerted prayer for revival.* For example, by serving the growing, multifaceted prayer movement in New York City, COPI hopes to see the Church within this world-class city influence the moral and spiritual life of the entire world. Our Message of Hope division also provides leadership and preaching missions for major conferences in countries around the world.

Upon request, COPI will provide a free ministry brochure and product catalogue that will explain more about Concerts of Prayer and the united prayer movement. Address your correspondence to:

Concerts of Prayer International (COPI)
P.O. Box 1399, Wheaton, IL 60189
Phone: (630) 690-8441
Fax: (630) 690-0160 • E-Mail: COPI@AOL.COM

FASTING FOR REVIVAL

BY BILL BRIGHT

BILL BRIGHT

Bill Bright is founder and president of Campus Crusade for Christ International with more than 14,000 full-time staff members. Dr. Bright is the recipient of many national and international awards, including five honorary doctorates. He was recently inducted into the Oklahoma Hall of Fame, and received the highly honored Templeton Award from the Queen of England.

If my people, which are called by my name, shall humble themselves, and pray, and seek my face, and turn from their wicked ways; then will I hear from heaven, and will forgive their sin, and will heal their land (2 Chron. 7:14, KJV).

During a 40-day fast, which God impressed me to undertake, I was seeking His guidance when something extraordinary happened. I distinctly sensed a sobbing in my spirit and, amazingly, I knew our Lord was weeping. I was startled at first. And although I did not know why He was weeping, I began to sob, too.

Then I sensed Him saying, "My people have forgotten one of the most important disciplines of the Christian life, the major key to revival." And I knew He meant fasting with prayer.

We can pray, witness, read the Word of God diligently, attend church, be active for Christ and aggressively do things to honor the Lord—all of which are commendable. But the major key to meeting the conditions of 2 Chronicles 7:14, the Holy Spirit was saying, is fasting. Certainly, we cannot fast and pray for a prolonged period of time without humbling ourselves and turning from our wicked ways.

WHAT IS REVIVAL?

Today, churches declare "revival" if they have a few exciting services. But revival is much more than that. Let us look briefly at some of its characteristics:

1. Revival is a sovereign act of God.
2. Revival is a divine visitation.
3. Revival is a time of personal humiliation, forgiveness and restoration in the Holy Spirit.
4. During revival, preaching is fearless under the anointing of the Holy Spirit—as in Acts 4:31 when "they spoke the word of God with boldness" (*NKJV*).
5. During revival the presence of the Holy Spirit is powerful.
6. Revival changes communities and nations.

Today, our decision is crucial as individuals, as a Church and as a nation. God is asking us to seek Him with all of our beings. The revival He promises begins when we humble ourselves, repent, fast, pray and seek His face and turn from our evil ways. God has promised to respond with revival fire for any person who will hear, love, trust and obey Him.

During my 40-day fast, the Holy Spirit assured me again and again that God will send a great revival to America and the world when His people heed His call to turn to Him, according to 2 Chronicles 7:14. I am confident that this awakening will result in the greatest spiritual harvest in history, and the Great Commission will be fulfilled in our generation.

HOW THE REVIVAL WILL COME

Revival comes as a sovereign act of God—as the result of Christian people meeting God's conditions by responding to the work of the Holy Spirit.

I believe three things must first happen before this revival can take place:

First, Christian leaders must catch the vision. They must play a prominent role in presenting the call of the Holy Spirit to their congregations.

WE NEED DEDICATED MINISTERS OF GOD WHO ARE NOT AFRAID TO CALL THEIR PEOPLE TO REPENTANCE—EVEN IF THIS RESULTS IN GREAT PERSONAL SACRIFICE.

I believe it is the duty of pastors to lead their people to repentance—by personal example as well as by proclamation. Joel records:

> O ministers of my God, lie all night before the altar, weeping....Announce a fast; call a solemn meeting. Gather the elders and all the people into the Temple of the Lord your God, and weep before him there. Alas, this terrible day of punishment is on the way. Destruction from the Almighty is almost here! (1:13-15, *TLB*).

We need dedicated ministers of God who are not afraid to call their people to repentance—even if this results in great personal sacrifice. Jonathan Edwards, for example, lost his pulpit when he put out his fiery call to repentance.

But other Christian leaders must also take up the banner. Broadcasters, heads of parachurch organizations, evangelists and influential lay leaders must all herald God's call.

Second, God's people must heed the call to repentance, fasting and prayer. As I have said, the promise of the coming revival carries one condition. Before God lifts His present hand of judgment from America, believers by the millions must first humble themselves and seek His face in fasting and prayer, according to 2 Chronicles 7:14.

Fasting is a biblical means of humbling ourselves, therefore, it is the only spiritual discipline that enables us to meet all the conditions of this passage.

Third, the Holy Spirit must convict the nation of its sins. No revival is possible without the convicting power of the Holy Spirit. Jesus said, "When [the Holy Spirit] comes, he will convict the world of guilt in regard to sin and righteousness and judgment" (John 16:8). As Christians humble themselves before the Lord, the Holy Spirit will convict people of their sins, cause them to repent, bring healing to His people and restore blessing to our land.

We have compiled a variety of materials to encourage you in developing a lifestyle of prayer and fasting. Currently, the three primary resources we offer are:

- *America's Call to Fast, Pray and Seek God's Face*
- *7 Basic Steps to Successful Fasting and Prayer*
- *How to Lead a Successful Fasting and Prayer Gathering*

Write to New Life Publications, which is a ministry of Campus Crusade for Christ, for a list of available materials:

New Life Publications
100 Sunport Lane
Orlando, FL 32809
CompuServe: 74114,1206
Internet: newlife@magicnet.net

FIVE ESSENTIALS FOR EFFECTIVE SPIRITUAL WARFARE

BY C. PETER WAGNER

C. PETER WAGNER

C. Peter Wagner has taught on the faculty of the Fuller Seminary School of World Missions for more than 25 years. He continues to teach church growth there, but has more recently assumed the additional role as Dean of Fuller Colorado, the extension center in Colorado Springs. Dr. Wagner is recognized as a leading authority in the field of spiritual warfare, and is the celebrated author of more than 30 books. He and his wife, Doris, are cofounders of the World Prayer Center. They are also members of New Life Church.

Almost every local church I know has had a burning desire to see its city change for the better. All too many of them, however, have been so discouraged that such desires are merely dim memories from the past. Why is this so common?

Many reasons exist. In this brief chapter, however, I want to focus on just one of them: *a low level of understanding about the nature of the spiritual warfare in which Christians are inevitably engaged.* Paul says, "lest Satan should take advantage of us...we are not ignorant of his devices" (2 Cor. 2:11, *NKJV*). This implies that if we *are* ignorant of Satan's devices to keep our cities in darkness, he will more than likely take advantage of us and fulfill his desire to steal, to kill and to destroy (see John 10:10).

THIS SHOULD NOT BE!

Almost every issue of the daily newspaper in virtually every city throughout the United States is replete with stories of stealing, killing and destroying—the works of the enemy. But this should not be! Why? "For this purpose the Son of God was manifested, that he might destroy the works of the devil" (1 John 3:8, *KJV*).

Fortunately, the decade of the 1990s has now become known as the "decade of spiritual warfare" within the Church. The Spirit has been speaking strongly to the churches about spiritual warfare, and those who have ears to hear are hearing what He is saying. Because of this, I have great hope that the condition of our cities will soon begin to change for the better. The very fact that two dynamic city pastors such as Ted Haggard and Jack Hayford have put together this cutting-edge book gives me renewed hope.

Books, tapes, conferences and even seminary courses about spiritual warfare are now plentiful. Pastors and other leaders are discussing this more than ever. Constructive criticism has sharpened our thinking. Bold pioneers have accumulated more and more frontline experience in engaging the enemy in their cities. They have learned both what to do and what not to do. The theory as well as the practices of spiritual warfare have matured considerably during recent years.

BREAKING THE STRONGHOLDS

As I have researched, written and taught about spiritual warfare, at least five essential elements for lasting effectiveness have surfaced. Although I cannot go into depth, I do feel it would be helpful to those planning strategies for reaching their cities for Christ to use them as a sort of checklist toward striving to break the hold of the forces of darkness over their communities.

1. Recognizing our authority. The Bible tells us we are ambassadors (see 2 Cor. 5:20). What differentiates an ambassador from the average citizen? Authority! Our ambassador to Japan, for example, has more authority there than most Americans because he comes "in the name of the president of the United States." By the same token, we go into enemy territory "in the name of Jesus Christ, the King of kings."

Jesus has given us the authority to use the keys of the kingdom of heaven to open the gates of Hades so His church will grow (see Matt. 16:18,19). What are these keys? "Whatever you bind on earth will be bound in heaven" (Matt. 16:19, *NKJV*). Jesus had already used the same verb when He taught His disciples that no one can enter a "strong man's house" unless he "binds the strong man" (Matt. 12:29, *NKJV*). All of this gives us a basis for understanding what Paul later wrote: "We wrestle not against flesh and blood, but against principalities, against powers" (Eph. 6:12, *KJV*).

How much authority has Jesus given us? More than many of us might think. He said to His disciples, "Behold, I give you the authority...over all the power of the enemy" (Luke 10:19, *NKJV*). There is little use considering spiritual warfare unless we understand all that is involved in being a true ambassador of God.

2. Developing the unity of Christian leaders. In the arena of a city, the pastors of local churches are the most important ambassadors of Christ: They are the highest spiritual authorities in the city. Jesus is the great shepherd of the sheep, and the pastors are His undershepherds. One of Satan's chief and most effective devices for keeping entire cities in darkness is to keep pastors apart from one another.

He doesn't necessarily make them enemies. He can accomplish his purpose just by keeping them indifferent toward one another. The Presbyterian pastor doesn't care much what the Nazarene pastor does. The white pastor doesn't care much what the black pastor does. The charismatic pastor doesn't care much what the traditional pastor does. The older established pastor doesn't care much what that young church planter does.

So Satan is happy. He can continue to steal, to kill and to destroy just by maintaining the status quo. He likes the churches in the city just the way they are: They are virtually no threat to him.

But Satan gets extremely worried when the pastors of a city begin to pray together regularly. The entire spiritual atmosphere starts to change. How such a thing can actually happen is eloquently described and analyzed in Ted Haggard's powerful book, *Primary Purpose* (Creation House). Why is this essential? Because Jesus prayed to the Father "that they may all be one...that the world may believe" (John 17:21, *NASB*). Experience shows that without the agreement of the pastors in the city's life-giving churches, the chances of engaging in effective spiritual warfare are slim.

3. Awareness of strategic timing. Many attempts at city-level spiritual warfare have come to naught because those attempting it have missed God's strategic timing. Authentic ambassadors do not make policies. They implement the policies made by the president. Likewise, we as servants of God do not make the policies, but we first discern what God wants us to do and when.

This is why it is so important for us to hear *The Voice of God*, to use the title of Cindy Jacobs's recent book. Jesus Himself did only what He saw the Father doing (see John 5:19). If such was necessary for Jesus, it is all the more necessary for us.

4. Precision in targeting. Why is it that in our churches we see frequent answers to our prayers for individuals and for families, but not to our prayers for the city? It is largely because when we pray for people, we first ask them what they want us to pray for, and we pray specifically for those things. We know from experience that the more specific our prayers, the more powerful they seem to be. Our problem is that we have not learned well how to ask similar questions to our city before we pray for it.

The relatively new science of "spiritual mapping" is helping us ask the right questions to our cities and to get the answers we need to target our prayers more accurately. In my book, *Breaking Strongholds in Your City* (Regal Books), such expert spiritual mappers as George Otis, Jr., Bob Beckett, Cindy Jacobs, Kjell Sjoberg, Harold Caballeros and others provide much of the information we need for intelligent targeting of our prayers.

5. Praying in the community. Traditionally, most of our praying has been done in our homes or in our churches or at times in Concerts of Prayer, bringing together people from many churches. We need to continue to do this and do it more. However, I believe that if we are going to be more effective in praying for our cities, we need also to do something else.

We need to move out from our churches and actually pray in our communities. God has given us four remarkable ways to implement this in recent years: (1) praise marches; (2) prayerwalking; (3) prayer journeys; and (4) prayer expeditions. All four of these methods are being practiced with great success by more and more believers. They are each described in detail in my book *Churches That Pray* (Regal Books), which I recommend for those who desire more information. This is the kind of prayer that has an extremely high potential to bring permanent change to a city.

Spiritual warfare is not an end in itself. It is simply one of the means toward the end of breaking the power of darkness over a city so the "god of this age" will no longer be able to "blind the minds" of those who do not yet believe in Jesus (see 2 Cor. 4:3,4). If we do it well we can accomplish, in Ted Haggard's words, "making it hard to go to hell from our city."

If you would like a catalog of books and tapes about spiritual warfare, you may contact:

The Arsenal
c/o Global Harvest Ministries
P.O. Box 63060
Colorado Springs, CO 80962-3060
Phone: (719)262-9929
Fax: (719)262-9920
E-Mail: 74114,570@compuserve.com

For information about the United Prayer Track of the A.D. 2000 and Beyond Movement, The World Prayer Center or Fuller Colorado, you may contact my office at Global Harvest Ministries at the previously mentioned numbers.

PRAYER EVANGELISM

BY ED SILVOSO

ED SILVOSO

After working for several years in crusade outreaches with his brother-in-law, evangelist Luis Palau, Ed Silvoso founded Harvest Evangelism to assist the Church in his native Argentina in reaching the entire nation for Christ. As a strategic thinker in the areas of evangelism and church planting, Ed and his team have developed a biblical prototype to reach entire cities for Christ, using prayer evangelism as the main tool. This prototype is being implemented in numerous cities on three continents. Ed Silvoso is also a graduate of Multnomah School of the Bible. He is the author of the popular book *That None Should Perish* (Regal Books). He and his wife, Ruth, and their four daughters live in San Jose, California.

Is it possible to reach an entire city for Christ? This was one of the first and most persistent questions I asked myself as a new believer. As a new Christian I had a weekly appointment with God. Week after week, as I watched the sun set on the Argentine pampas, I begged

God to send us a touch of revival, and as part of that, to allow Christians to reach an entire city for Christ.

PLAN RESISTENCIA

I remember the day our team from Harvest Evangelism met with the pastors of Resistencia, a city in Argentina, to officially suggest a plan for evangelizing their city. "Plan Resistencia" was an acknowledgment of God's love for the lost in the city and the Church's commitment to the biblical principles of unity, holiness and prayer.

We challenged the pastors to establish a perimeter of godliness in the city. They did this by meeting regularly for prayer, intercession and accountability. This was an auspicious beginning in a city of about 400,000 where we were told 68 of the 70 existing congregations were the result of church splits. Yet, the Holy Spirit began to work in

THERE IS ONLY ONE CHURCH IN THE CITY THAT MEETS IN MANY DIFFERENT CONGREGATIONS.

the pastors' lives as they met, and soon a deep bond of love had completely enveloped them.

Let me touch on the highlights of the plan. In essence, Plan Resistencia was the implementation of Paul's instructions to Timothy as recorded in 1 Timothy 2:1-8. The Church was to consistently and systematically pray for everybody in the city—especially for those in authority—with the clear intent of seeing all of them saved.

This was to be done with holy hands, for it is necessary to first rid the Church of division and dissension. This was also to be done by following Paul's outline in Ephesians 2-6, where the Church is exhorted to restore unity by dealing with ethnic disunity, church disunity, ministerial disunity, marital disunity and family and workplace disunity before engaging "the spiritual forces of wickedness in the heavenly places" (6:12, *NASB*).

It was agreed among the participating pastors that there is only one Church in the city that meets in many different congregations. As such, the pastors must see themselves as undershepherds serving under the only Chief Shepherd, Jesus Himself, and the various congregations in town must see themselves as part of, and interdependent upon, the other congregations. The main reason for the Church's presence on earth is to have its members conformed to the image of God's Son and, as a result of that, to take the gospel to everyone in the city. To do this effectively, the Church must deal with longstanding issues of disunity, expressed through wrath and dissension.

EVICTING SATANIC PRINCIPALITIES

All of these steps take place in the context of active spiritual warfare where the Church constantly struggles against rulers, against the world forces of this darkness, against the spiritual forces of wickedness in the heavenly places (see Eph. 6:12). The essence of this struggle is twofold. The Church must "put on the full armor of God, that [it] may be able to stand firm against the schemes of the devil" (Eph. 6:11, *NASB*). On the other hand, the Church must also invade Satan's territory, mainly through intercessory prayer.

To do this, the pastors in Resistencia began to pray together regularly. They exchanged pulpits. They sent love offerings to needy congregations. They brought their people together to celebrate their newfound unity in Christ. Peter and Doris Wagner and Cindy Jacobs taught scores of leaders and pastors about intercession and spiritual warfare. Hundreds of intercessors were recruited, equipped and deployed throughout the city to secure and expand God's "beachhead" there.

Satan's perimeter was infiltrated by 635 neighborhood prayer cells (called "lighthouses") scattered throughout the city. Little by little, every home in the city received prayer. Answered prayers gave the Church favor in the eyes of the people. "Spiritual IOUs" began to pile up in 635 neighborhoods.

Satan's perimeter began to be shaken when the pastors and their most trusted intercessors proclaimed the lordship of Christ by serving an eviction notice on the city's satanic principality San La Muerte, which means "Saint Death." Pastors and leaders suffered all kinds of attacks. However, God was in control and He showed it. At the height of the conflict, San La Muerte's high priestess died in strange circumstances: The mattress she was sleeping on caught fire and burned her to death. Nothing else burned except her body, the bed and the idol of San La Muerte in the room next door! The fear of God fell upon the city.

Taking advantage of the extensive and intensive prayer ministry of more than 600 neighborhood prayer cells, two major outreaches were executed. First, in one day the entire city (approximately 63,000 homes) was visited with a good news package, which was made available by Every Home for Christ Crusade. The week before, the city was blitzed through TV with the announcement that the following Saturday "This package of good news is coming to your home." Eventually every home in the city was blessed.

The same night after the good news packages arrived, the people of Resistencia were invited to go to a covered stadium to thank God for His blessings. The mayor was there to thank us. The media covered the event. The slogan for the outreach was, "Resistencia, it is God's time for you."

POSITIONING FOR POWER

The second evangelistic event consisted of a series of simultaneous crusades; 34 small neighborhood crusades and; three months later, 10 larger area crusades. Finally, a citywide crusade was conducted. By working out of the more than 600 lighthouses, the idea was to expand from the micro to the macro picture. By the time of the citywide crusade, the city was totally open, and Satan was raving mad.

On the opening night of the citywide crusade, we discovered that the local witches and warlocks had occupied the corner of the field. Satan had launched an all-out counterattack. We positioned our top intercessors under the platform along with a ring of 70 others around the podium. Approximately 100 more mixed in the crowd.

Thousands of people came to the Lord. The challenge of following through with them in their new faith was made easier by the hundreds of lighthouses spread out all around the city. The mayor acknowledged Jesus Christ as his Savior. Later, two of the candidates for governor prayed to receive Jesus into their hearts. Also, medical doctors, journalists, one senator, an alderman, politicians and lawyers responded. The city had indeed heard the voice of God!

When the evangelistic phase ended, the pastors moved on to establish God's perimeter where Satan's used to be. In military terms, when raiding the enemy's camp, you transform his stronghold by occupying it and turning the guns around. Satan's stronghold within the Church had been division, fed by deep mistrust. This time the pastors targeted unity and trust. Six months later, a church census was taken and the Church had grown 102 percent.

FINALLY, AN ENTIRE CITY REACHED FOR CHRIST

The pastors of Resistencia had given the Church-at-large a unique gift: a model for effective evangelism. They allowed God to prove that cities can and must be entirely reached for Christ. Resistencia is not a perfect example. It is simply a prototype. By 1994, 16 other cities in three continents were applying many of the principles pioneered in Resistencia.

On the day I left Resistencia, the plane took off toward the east, flying over the Parana River, which 700 kilometers further south washes the beaches of my native San Nicolas. This is the river that quietly listened to my youthful conversations with God week after week. Thirty years had passed, and, finally, I had seen an entire city reached for Christ. Now we must perfect the prototype and make it available to the nations.

For more information, write to or call:

Rev. Ed Silvoso, Director
Harvest Evangelism
P.O. Box 20310
San Jose, CA 95160-0310
Phone: (408) 927-9052

PRAYERWALKING: SATURATING YOUR CITY WITH PRAYER

BY STEVE HAWTHORNE

STEVE HAWTHORNE

Steve Hawthorne is the director of WayMakers, a ministry focused on united, citywide prayer. He is best known as one of the designers of the mission vision course called *Perspectives on the World Christian Movement*. Steve has coauthored, with Graham Kendrick, the book *Prayerwalking: Praying On-Site with Insight*. He has trained teams in on-site prayer in a dozen countries. Steve Hawthorne is a member of Hope Chapel in Austin, Texas.

God is rousing Christians to pray for their cities in an "up close and personal" way. We are seeing Christians press their prayers beyond the walls of church buildings to bring clear and quiet blessings upon their neighbors in Jesus' name. As they put feet to their prayers, God helps turn their fresh hope into obedient action.

PRAYERWALKING: PRAYING ON-SITE WITH INSIGHT

We've come to call this sort of on-site intercession "prayerwalking." It is simply praying in the very places we expect God to bring forth His answers.

The prayers are intercessory rather than devotional. Prayerwalkers learn to pray beyond their own concerns, focusing prayer on behalf of their neighbors.

Prayerwalking is usually a low-profile affair: Friends or family strolling two-by-two through their own neighborhoods, schools and work places, praying as they go. It's being on the scene without making one.

CITYWIDE WALKS: COORDINATING TO COVER THE COMMUNITY

Most prayerwalking has been sporadic and scattered, as Christians pray occasionally for a few neighbors during morning walks. We encourage those prayers, but we are now seeing a rise of organized citywide prayerwalks designed to saturate entire cities. Plans are varied and creative. Every community seems to require a unique approach. Sometimes God inspires the vision to the people of one church. More often, many churches find they share common hope and mission on the (literally) common ground of their streets.

ONE-DAY PRAYERWALKS AT KEY SITES

Some communities have used a one-day approach, arranging routes that symbolically cover the entire city. "PrayerWalk Nashville '95" was this kind of effort. On a September Saturday morning, Christians from 29 Nashville churches gathered quietly at 32 preplanned sites along Old Hickory Boulevard, which encircles the core of the city as a "ring road." At 9:00 A.M. 32 groups (usually comprised of folks from the same church) began to move counterclockwise along preassigned routes. They gathered afterward for a time of celebration. Even more churches joined as they expanded the effort the following year.

In Los Angeles hundreds of churches participated in what was called "Lift LA" during mid-November, 1995. In conjunction with a call to prayer and fasting, organizers helped local church leaders plan three successive mornings of prayerwalking. Scores of teams set out on short prayerwalks they had planned—most synchronized to depart at 5:00 A.M.

I was able to join in the endeavor. Our assigned route: Hollywood Boulevard. As we walked along the brass stars embedded in the sidewalk during the morning dark, it wasn't hard to plead for God's light to dawn anew, eclipsing the seductive starlight of our idolatrous entertainment industry. How thrilled we were to know that at that very hour, hundreds of others were putting feet to their prayers all around the city.

COMPREHENSIVE PRAYERWALKS

Some citywide prayerwalks aim to cover every street or even every home. We recently completed an effort such as this in Austin, Texas, called "PrayerWalk Austin." We called Christians to prayerwalk every street in the city during the 24 days between Halloween and Thanksgiving, 1995.

We divided the map of Austin into 740 small sectors, each requiring about an hour to cover. We invited Christians to register for two of the numbered sectors: one area near their home, work or church; and a second sector in a part of Austin they didn't often see. We invited participants to find their own styles and schedules to prayerwalk their areas anytime, but at least once during the 24-day period. We kept it simple. No literature was distributed. We just asked God to bring the transforming power of the gospel to every home, school and business. We closed the event with a citywide Thanksgiving celebration on the Friday evening after Thanksgiving Day.

Christians from 70 churches had prayerwalked the city. The walk had been accomplished with minimal publicity, a steering committee of pastors and an eager volunteer team. More than 58 percent of the map had been assigned to prayerwalkers in a short time.

THE NEXT STEP

The next step is probably near where you live, work or worship. With a friend, pray with biblical hope for the families, educators, leaders and children of your community. It's so simple that you can start tomorrow. Focus on Christ, asking Him to fulfill all of His heart for every neighborhood. As you find creative, persistent ways to bless your neighbors in Jesus' name, you will be among the first to see God's hand at work in their lives.

Many are recognizing God's timing to organize citywide prayerwalks. March for Jesus, USA has lifted a vision called "Prayerwalk USA" seeking to strengthen local efforts by providing resources and referrals. PrayerWalk USA will help local leaders encourage and fortify each other, suggesting common approaches for coverage and publishing reports of progress. A *PrayerWalk Organizer Guide* (prepared by WayMakers) is available. It is designed to help local church leaders develop customized plans to prayerwalk their cities.

Many hearts share our hope to cover every community in America with prayer—street by street, home by home. Why not aim to cover every zip code with prayer at least once by the year 2000? Eventually we may see every home upheld in prayer daily by caring Christian neighbors: Step by step....Street by street....Family by family.

As we bring our prayers near our neighbors, we will prepare the way for gospel harvest and Christ's greater glory.

For information about organizing a prayerwalk in your city, contact:

WayMakers
Box 20 3131
Austin, TX 78720-3131
Phone: (512) 419-7729
Fax: (512) 219-1999

Plan Together

CLEARLY MARKING THE TARGET

BY TED HAGGARD

ELLIOTT HAGGARD

A shovelful of horse manure slammed into Elliott's face. He stood there shocked and...after a moment of apprehensive silence, broke into laughter. With only his two eyes and little mouth as bastions of purity, my three-year-old son demonstrated his strength of character while covered in dung.

He knew I didn't intentionally want to hit him with manure as we cleaned the stables together, and he had the personal self-confidence to see the humor in the midst of the repulsive smell. He grew a foot taller in the eyes of his family that day. So tall, in fact, that he resisted his mother's attempts to wash his face. He proudly wore the caked-on muck as proof of his manhood. Because he knew exactly where he stood in his relationships within the family, he knew how to respond to a dirty face.

Later that day, as the go-cart spun out of control, slamming into the side of the barn, Elliott's chin dripped blood as our stunned guests grabbed him and swiftly carried him into the house. In Elliott's love for adventure, he had quietly slipped into the driver's seat of the idling go-cart and pressed the accelerator as far as his three-year-old legs could reach.

Unable to steer or control the speed, Elliott soon discovered a relationship between excitement and pain. After a tearful moment when I applied hydrogen peroxide and a Spiderman Band-Aid, Elliott returned boldly to the party with the poise of a decorated soldier. Because he knew how others would view him, he knew he could return to the party in confidence.

The next day Elliott was in the center of the backseat with his older brother Marcus (13) on one side and his sister Christy (14) on the other. Laughing and talking, Christy playfully commented that Elliott's fingers looked stubby. His countenance fell as he studied his little hands. Bewildered by the comparison of his hands to those of his brother and sister, he discovered they were right. He, like all three-year-olds, did have stubby fingers. His heart sank. He *was* defective. Sorrow overtook him.

Elliott didn't have any way of knowing if his fingers were stubby for a three-year-old. He had never thought about his fingers before, so anything anyone said about them was true. Because he had no way of knowing the truth, he believed and responded to something that was not true. He thought he had stubby fingers. The forlorn expression on his face reflected his sinking heart as he studied his hands.

From the driver's seat, I asked to see his hands. Christy felt terrible and longed for Elliott's emotional rescue. I looked at his hands and assured him that his fingers were perfectly normal. Christy immediately jumped in and said she remembered her fingers looking just like his when she was three. Elliott smiled, examined his hands with confidence and was back to his usual man-child self.

ACCURATE INFORMATION IN, ACCEPTABLE RESPONSES OUT

Elliott is just like we are in many ways. When we have accurate information like Elliott had (knowing that he was okay even with a dirty face and a bloodied chin), we know what to do. Without accurate information, though, we develop wrong conclusions and are more likely to do the wrong things. In the last example regarding his fingers, he didn't have enough information to evaluate himself accurately nor to determine an acceptable response.

That is exactly where we are in most cities. We are lacking enough accurate information to determine acceptable responses.

To be increasingly effective in the mega-cities of the world, Dr. Jack Dennison, the U.S. Regional Director for DAWN ministries, an expert on impacting cities through local church growth, suggests that all Christian movements thoughtfully answer three questions:

1. Where are we?
2. Where are we going?
3. How do we get there from here?

Obviously, we have measurement systems in each of our churches that assist us in answering these questions. To assess where we are, we can look at our budgets, attendance records, asset accumulations and other indicators of our current ministry effectiveness (or at least size).

At any time I [Ted Haggard] can tell you how we are financially as a church, how many tapes were distributed last week, how many people attended cell groups and how many people our outreach efforts are affecting in the community and overseas. Yes, we in the local church have measurement systems to know where we are!

It is the role of the senior pastor and his leadership team to establish clear direction for the local church. For example, I believe New Life Church, the church I pastor in Colorado Springs, will ultimately be a church that services 20,000 people. In addition, I believe the overall Body of Christ in Colorado Springs will continue to grow and that the young people and the resources of our city will be used in global evangelization. That is where we are going.

But how do we get there? New Life Church has five strategic objectives that provide parameters for everything we do:

1. We have Sunday services where people can freely worship God and study the Scriptures.
2. We emphasize Christian education for young people (newborn through college age).

3. We highlight leadership development (discipleship) through an extensive cell-group system.
4. We pray for the unreached, and then endeavor to reach the unreached that are within our reach.
5. We encourage harmony among pastors and churches in order to advance evangelism. (That is why I am writing this book.)

Let me emphasize: This is *all* we do. Therefore, we are protected from getting distracted and losing our effectiveness. If something comes up that doesn't fit into these five objectives, we don't do it. We don't randomly do anything. We are purposeful.

So, as a local church, we are able to assess where we are, where we are going and how we are going to get there.

Even though we are able to establish these reference points as local churches, we have previously not been adequately motivated to do the same thing in our cities. Recently, however, the Holy Spirit has been directing Christian leaders throughout the world to implement citywide partnerships to ensure that everyone in the city has an opportunity to respond positively to the gospel.

These new citywide partnerships require new measurement systems. Currently, most communities have no way of measuring where we are as a Body of believers. Nor do most of us have any mechanism for establishing where the Lord wants us to go. Thus, the question of How do we get there? receives a random answer at best. Many times we try to get "there," without established targets. As a result, we can only hope our attempts at communicating the gospel will actually hit a target...any target...somewhere...somehow.

READY, SHOOT, AIM

Rick Warren illustrates this lack of aim in his excellent book *The Purpose Driven Church*, when he writes,

> I once saw a Peanuts cartoon that described the evangelistic strategy of many churches. Charlie Brown was practicing archery in his backyard. Instead of aiming at a target, he would shoot an arrow at his fence and then

walk over and draw a target around wherever the arrow stuck. Lucy walked up and said, "Why are you doing this, Charlie Brown?"

He replied without embarrassment, "This way I never miss!"

Rick drives the point home by adding:

Unfortunately the same logic is behind a lot of churches' evangelistic outreach efforts. We shoot arrows of good news into our community and if they happen to hit anyone we say, "That was our target all along!" There is little planning or strategy behind our efforts—we don't aim at any specific target. We just draw a bull's-eye around whomever we reach and settle for that. This is an incredibly callous approach to evangelism. Bringing people to Christ is too important a task for us to have such a casual attitude toward it.[1]

Rick's book teaches local churches how to identify their targets for ministry and develop strategies to achieve their goals. His book is a must for every Christian leader. *Loving Your City into the Kingdom* could be viewed as an adaptation of Rick's thoughts for applying them to cities. Groups of successful churches in strategic partnerships can transform entire communities with the gospel.

In the first three chapters of this book, we have established the benefits of praying together. As we have already discussed, one of those benefits is the establishment of vision. God's vision gives us parameters that help us answer the question, Where are we going? In this chapter, we will further explore answers to these questions:

- Where are we now?
- Where are we going?
- How do we get there from here?

WHERE ARE WE NOW?

We must do three things to understand where we are within our cities: (1) accumulate historical research to help us understand why things are as they are; (2) evaluate current attitudes and trends; and

(3) create a simple spiritual map so everyone can easily picture our city and our corporate witness as it is right now.

PEOPLE AFFECTED BY THE WORK OF THE HOLY SPIRIT ARE CHANGED, AND CHANGED PEOPLE CHANGE THEIR BEHAVIOR. WHEN ENOUGH PEOPLE IN A COMMUNITY CHANGE THEIR BEHAVIOR, THEIR SOCIETY CHANGES.

Historical Overview
The following sample questions can be helpful for establishing some of the history that influences your city:

1. What civilizations lived in your city before the present one, and did they participate in any questionable religious practices that could still be affecting people?
2. Who were the founders of the modern culture of your city, and what did they believe? (Orlando, Salt Lake City and Mecca all have very different spiritual histories because the fathers of their modern cultures had very different spiritual perspectives.)
3. What does the name of your city mean?
4. What do the symbols in your city's seal and flag represent?
5. What power points and high places in your city have a history of spiritual activity?
6. Does your city conduct any festivals or community celebrations that are displeasing to the Lord?
7. Are there specific points in history that have caused a dramatic shift in the direction of your city?
8. Do any old divisions between Bible-believing Christian groups linger there?

From these answers, you will uncover issues that require intercession. You may also discover some understanding of why some people in your city believe and behave as they do.

Current Attitudes and Trends

The following survey questions can be used to compile an overview of the attitudes in your city. They are all yes or no questions so percentages can be calculated from the results.

City Attitudes. (To conduct a more extensive survey, you could create a segment survey from this. After identifying which segment of your city the person you are speaking to is a part of, incorporate his or her answers into a matrix of "segment attitudes.")

1. Are Christians good or bad?
2. Is there any one true religion?
3. Is Jesus Christ the son of God?
4. Does the Church help or hurt society?
5. Is the Bible God's supreme Word to people?
6. Do demons really exist?
7. Are angels real?
8. Does God offer you a guaranteed way to go to heaven?
9. Is there a judgment after death?
10. Is there eternal life?
11. Is there heaven for some and hell for others after death?
12. Would you ever encourage a friend to have an abortion?
13. Is homosexuality equally as acceptable as heterosexuality?
14. Do people need forgiveness from God?
15. Is it OK to be sexually active with another person outside of or before marriage?

Societal Trends. The Spirit of God working in a community affects people. People affected by the work of the Holy Spirit are changed, and changed people change their behavior. When enough people in a community change their behavior, their society changes. Gauging societal trends can be an excellent way to determine the effectiveness of the church's corporate witness within your community.

CHAPTER FOUR

1. What is your city's current crime rate? Has it risen or fallen in the last three years?
2. What is the current teen-pregnancy rate? Has it risen or fallen in the last three years?
3. How many people in your city have filed for divorce each year for the last three years? What is the trend?
4. What is the median educational level of the people in your city? (Is it rising or lowering? Compare this answer with the median educational level in the churches.)
5. What are the ethnic groups represented in your city, and what percentage of the population do they account for? (This is meaningful if you discover an ethnic group that either does not have many life-giving churches, or is not represented within the integrated church community.)
6. What is the median age of the people in your city? Is it rising or lowering? How do these age groups compare with the age groups in the church population? (Many cities have an increasingly younger population while the church community is aging.)

This list of questions should be customized for your own community. Don't be afraid to ask hard questions, especially the ones that might make you look bad. A measurement is only as honest as the scale by which it is taken.

Our City and Our Witness

To visually see where you are and tangibly monitor progress, a spiritual map of your city is an invaluable tool. Just as road maps are marked by the location of roads, and topographical maps make special notes about elevations, so spiritual maps identify spiritually sensitive locations in a city. George Otis, Jr. has generated some of the finest material available for spiritual mapping. It is fundamental to accurate assessment and implementation of citywide gospel presentation. Before reading his material, though, the following provides an elementary overview of spiritual mapping. It will give you a starting point that can be built upon later.

Constructing a Simple Spiritual Map

1. Find a large city map that can be placed on a wall or some other easily accessible location.
2. Place a like-colored dot on the map for every church in the city. Watch for concentrations of churches, or areas void of local churches.
3. Place other colored dots on the map for elementary, middle and high schools. Also locate community colleges and universities.
4. Mark government buildings on the map.
5. Identify the locations of sources for demonic influence in your city (bars, dance clubs, porno shops, sexually-oriented bath houses, etc.).
6. Identify sources of gross spiritual deception such as New Age bookstores, Unitarian/Universalist churches, Mormon churches, Christian Science Reading Rooms, locations used for occult activities, spiritism, palm readers, etc.

With this map, you will be able to quickly see geographical areas of opportunity in your city. This research will prove that the life-giving churches working together are our only hope of substantively serving our cities for the gospel. I don't know of any major metropolitan cities that have been measurably impacted by one successful church—it takes a group of successful churches!

Updating this map every six months will also provide a simple method for measuring effectiveness. For example, if the number of churches is increasing and the number of bars and porno joints is decreasing, that is positive and should foster a sense of motivation within the Church Body to do even more. If the opposite trend occurs, it should be a warning that additional outreach is needed. It serves as a call to arms for the Body, and a need to take a more offensive position.

Measuring Our Corporate Witness

Now that we understand our history and some of the conditions in our city, we must accurately assess how we, the Church, are working within our city. Our goal is to meaningfully assess the level of our corporate witness in the community. Then, as we implement local church-based strategies to win the lost, we can easily evaluate our successes and shortcomings.

1. What is the population of your city?
2. How many Bible-believing churches exist in your city?
3. What is the average attendance of those churches?
4. What is the membership of those churches?
5. What is the median age of those who attend?
6. What is the median educational level of those who attend those churches?
7. In the last three years, which churches are growing, declining or level in attendance? (Calculate whether or not churches are growing, declining or level in overall attendance citywide. This data is crucial because it reflects the condition of the pool of church attendees citywide.)
8. *Estimate* what percentage of the churches in your city are life giving. (A life-giving church is one that effectively communicates Jesus Christ as the only solution to mankind's sin problem and the Bible as God's guide for our faith and practice. The key, though, is that life-giving churches communicate from His Spirit of Life, not the haughtiness of legalism nor the compromise of liberalism.) Remember, only estimate here. **Do not** make a list of life-giving and nonlife-giving churches because that list will undercut your ability to work in your city at large.
9. Calculate the percentage of people that are in life-giving churches on an average Sunday morning. (Christmas and Easter don't count.)

With these questions answered, you will gain the information necessary to compare the Church Body with the city at large.

The answer to question 9 is what I call "the water level of the Holy Spirit's activity in the city," or the Church's corporate witness. For an in-depth list of key questions, please see the following resources:

1. *Spiritual Mapping Field Guide* (Lynnwood, WA: The Sentinel Group, 1993), and

2. *Studying Your Community* by Rolland L. Warren (New York: Free Press Division of MacMillian Publishing Company).

The ongoing process of your research effort must result in cycles of research, planning, implementation and evaluation and then a redirection of your ministry. The following diagram shows the application of this fine-tuning ministry aid.

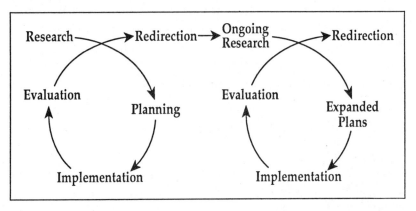

Now that you know where you are, you, as a strategic alliance of life-giving churches, can develop a corporate direction to pursue in your community.

WHERE ARE WE GOING?

The process of establishing direction can easily bog down in too many good ideas and lofty dreams. In chapters 2 and 3 I discussed praying together as a foundational step because in the midst of prayer comes an easily defined vision for the city. Then, with His vision and the relationships that form in the midst of prayer movements, a simple answer to the question, Where are we going? can emerge.

For example, simple goals like:

- We want to pray for each person in the city, individually, at least once this year.
- We want to communicate the gospel, in an understandable way, to every person in our city at least once a year.
- We want to raise the water level of the Holy Spirit's

activity (the gauge of our corporate witness) in our city 1 percent a year for the next 10 years.

Done. It's simple, easy to read and understand. But these goals require broad-based cooperation of churches and the expertise of servant ministries to be accomplished. We must remove our spiritual blindfolds and take aim. Together we can hit this target. It doesn't move or change. And when we aim with purpose and power, we help people find heaven and avoid hell. It's not overly theological, nor does it bog down in technical terms. Instead, our strategies just provide a goal, a framework to set direction and motivation.

HOW DO WE GET THERE?

Utilize Diversity

I am writing today in Denver, Colorado. Earlier today I met some young people, ages 14 to 19, who live on the streets here. Before introducing myself, I observed them for an hour. During that time they didn't do anything but sit and stare into the air. Walking past them were business executives, college students and street vendors, but these street kids were oblivious to others. When a friend would walk up, they welcomed each other with hand motions—never a handshake. When a lover would approach, the greeting would be extremely sexual. When the police would pass, these youths would call them names.

As I watched, hundreds of questions rushed through my mind. I approached them explaining that I was writing this book and had a few questions for them. They ignored me. I sat down on the bench beside them and gazed into the same silent space they were staring into. (What a sight. These kids were all "grunge" kids with rings in everything, black dog collars around their necks and multiple hair colors, while I'm a clean-cut preppie. Clash!) Anyway, after about an hour, a friend of theirs approached and they introduced me. Then another came along with a similar introduction. Two hours of sitting on a bench in complete silence passed before one of the 18-year-olds said, "OK, we'll tell you what you want to know." And a fascinating conversation followed.

They have their own language and hand-signal communication

system. More than half do not have a home and live exclusively on the streets. Some are prostitutes, both male and female, but most beg for money to survive. The church is a place to get free food, but they have no idea what a "Christian" is. Jesus is a baby, work is a bother and police are a hassle. A street preacher comes by regularly in his suit to tell them they are going to hell; but they already know that, and obviously have never been able to hear the good news from him. They ignore him. He's irrelevant.

As I tried to talk with these kids about their futures, goals, ambi-

WE MUST BE LIKE JESUS AND SPEAK ABOUT SHEEP TO SHEPHERDS; SEED TIME AND HARVEST TO FARMERS; JUDGMENT TO OUR MODERN-DAY, SELF-APPOINTED RELIGIOUS WATCHDOGS; AND FORGIVENESS AND HEALING TO THE SINNERS.

tions, etc., they looked at me like I like I was speaking in a foreign language. Everything I suggested was completely new to them. We thought on two very different levels. I thought in terms of their eternity; they thought in terms of escaping the hopelessness and boredom of today. I thought in terms of their eternal relationships; they cared only about the acceptance of their friends. Jobs, careers, education, families and other ideas were of no interest. None of them expected to be alive a year from today. I felt foolish bringing up subjects concerning the future. Their attitudes and values were totally different from mine.

The clash of values, attitudes and cultures prevented the good news from being heard from traditional sources. If we expect to communicate effectively, we must be like Jesus and speak about sheep to shepherds; seed time and harvest to farmers; judgment to our modern-day, self-appointed religious watchdogs; and forgiveness and healing to the sinners. We must communicate His good news in a way that can be easily understood. One of the reasons God sent Jesus to show us Himself in human form is so we could understand by seeing, and duplicate ministry by modeling. So too, our modern cities need that same opportunity. We need to know them before we can speak a language they can understand.

Just as there are specific people groups with their own languages and cultures in foreign missions projects, so each of our major cities have groups of people with their own languages and cultures. The kids who live on the streets speak a different language than the executives working in offices above them.

Some of these groups are "unreached people groups." Others of them have a significant Christian population. For example, in Colorado Springs, we discovered a strong Christian presence among our doctors, but a minimal percentage of our engineers knew the Lord. Thus, we needed to develop a strategy to reach engineers.

For some cities, to be effective we need to know how many Islamic, Hindu or Buddhist people live in the city. Where do they meet? How do they live? How can we communicate with and pray for them? Those of us from university towns need to know how many foreign students are in our cities and where they are from. Others of us need to know the inmate population. Once we know them, we can help them to know Christ.

Build Strategic Alliances

And that is why Jesus has such a diverse Body. Through alliances we can utilize our theological and cultural differences to communicate the gospel message in our diverse cities. If we want to impact society, we have no choice. but to capitalize on the strength of our differences—and that is only possible if we partner.

These alliances are not based on tolerating each other's differences, nor do they advocate compromise. Instead, they transform our differences into the strengths that, I believe, Jesus intends them to be—just as the differences between our eyes and our legs help us when they work in harmony. To function, however, neither our eyes nor our legs need to compromise or change. On the contrary! They actually need to do what they do well, with a willingness to communicate so their overall effectiveness is enhanced. It is only because of that dynamic that we can throw a ball, carry something into another room or drive a car. Only when the various portions of the Body of

Christ work in their different capacities can the Lord actually make us one, as He and the Father are one.

One church, one style of churches (a denomination or even a group of cessationist evangelical churches or exclusively Pentecostal/charismatic churches) is not diverse or strong enough to shift the societal norm of a city. Only broad-based groupings of churches humbled through prayer and directed by Scripture can work strategically as a unified Body to ensure the clear communication of the gospel to all. Utilizing the diversity of the Body is our only hope. Our differences are our strength.

NOW HIT THE TARGET

In the last two chapters about prayer we established the need to have God's vision for your city. In addition, we highlighted the necessity for healthy relationships among the Christians in the city enabling His Body to function effectively. Now, in this chapter and the one following, we have discussed how to identify the targets for ministry: the people groups of your city. With these resources, you now know how to identify where you are as a Body of believers in relation to the task at hand, where you are going and how you're going to get there.

So let's do it! Let's *mount up* in unity and prayer as a strong Body. Let's *march out* as informed Christian troops focused on His target. And let's *move in* to those targeted areas with ministries that heal and help hurting people. We must strategically target the most unreached people groups of the community and enable life-giving ministries to penetrate those groups with the gospel.

As we hear God's voice, we can answer the heart cry of His creation in a language they can hear and respond to.

Note
1. Rick Warren, *The Purpose Driven Church* (Grand Rapids: Zondervan, 1995), p. 155.

5

RESOURCES FOR "PLANNING TOGETHER"

DISCOVERING YOUR CITYWIDE STRATEGIES

CONTRIBUTORS:

PHILL BUTLER	JAAN HEINMETS
TONY EVANS	GEORGE BARNA
GEORGE OTIS, JR.	JACK L. DENNISON

Six outstanding pioneers in developing strategies for communities have contributed to this chapter. All of these writers are committed to the Great Commission and to the strengthening of the local church. As you read through the following articles, remember that each section is like a menu item. You may want to use the resources offered immediately, or you may want to wait.

You will know what is right for your community. It is vitally important, though, that you are aware of the resources available to the Body of Christ as you seek the growth of His kingdom.

After reading this chapter, you will see that each of the strategies presented have something to offer all of us.

We've learned about the necessity of *praying together.*

Now we're learning the necessity of *planning together.*

In chapters six and seven we'll learn how to implement our strategies by *going together.*

STRATEGIC PARTNERSHIP: THE BODY OF CHRIST IN ACTION

BY PHILL BUTLER

PHILL BUTLER

Phill Butler has been president of Interdev since 1974. He is chairman of the Task Force for Partnership Development of the A.D. 2000 and Beyond Movement, and has ministered in more than 80 countries. He has worked as an international radio and television correspondent and a communications consultant with governmental and nonprofit agencies in 4 countries. Phill has published more than 50 articles about strategic alliances.

Strategic partnership with churches and other ministries in your city can help you achieve your vision and succeed in your ministry.

Built wisely, partnership is a Spirit-fueled engine for expanded power and impact that God promises to bless.

What is a "strategic partnership"?

Partnership:
> Any group of individuals or organizations who commit themselves to work together in some way to fulfill a common purpose. (Example: Four churches decide to go together to build and operate a common youth center in the inner city, which none of them could do individually.)

Partners often operate at a high level of consensus, with personal trust and relationships as key elements in their long-term success. Each has to own the vision, believe in the process, believe in the other participants and see the benefits to his or her own congregation.

Overseas, in missions, a trend is growing toward integrating different ministries with a focus on one people group. These initiatives are being called "Strategic Evangelism Partnerships."

- *Strategic* because the partnership looks at the big picture—all the major factors and players involved in reaching a particular people, nation or city.
- *Evangelism* because the ultimate goal is the full fruit of evangelism, a vibrant local church.

- *Partnership* because even though the various ministries retain their own identities, each has a part, coordinating their strengths with those of different strengths (such as linking radio with both literature and village evangelists) for maximum total influence.

What if you applied this kind of approach to others of like faith in an area two miles around your church building?

WHY SHOULD I PARTNER WITH ANYBODY?

Partnership Is Biblical. It is God's way for God's blessing!

- God lives in community, in relationship. Partnership in ministry is in His image, His pattern.
- The gospel is the good news of restored relationships, and partnerships demonstrate that restoration—to God and to other men and women.
- Jesus linked our credibility with the unbelieving world to our oneness in Him (see John 17:21). The spiritual reality of oneness in Christ is more believable with the practical, visible reality of cooperation among believers.
- The Body in action is partnership in modern terms. It is like those described in Ephesians 4, Romans 12 and 1 Corinthians 12. (Sharing together with other believers—in resources, in struggles, in service—is God's directive for the *process* of Body ministry.)
- Blessings from God, such as spiritual power and refreshment, are for believers who dwell together in unity (see Ps. 133).

Partnership Is Practical. It can make us more effective because it:

- Saves money;
- Reduces duplication;
- Builds morale, especially among technicians or specialists who often don't see or sense their vital contributions to the final part in the whole of ministry—changing lives;

- Plugs holes (the gaps inevitable for a ministry working alone) that people fall through;
- Multiplies our resources;
- Encourages wholistic ministry by integrating special-ties that allow each person and each ministry to do what they do best. By integrating different strengths, all are contributing to a more effective overall outreach;
- Increases power and credibility for effectiveness (see John 17:23).

It works.

How to Work in Partnership

Interdev has 10 years of experience in helping to form and maintain effective ministry partnerships. That experience covers several conti-nents, with more than 160 ministries from both western and non-western countries. From this background and consultations with oth-ers who have tried ministry partnerships, some patterns have emerged that can help you find your way. Partnership is not a mys-terious black box anymore. The following reveals what is inside.

Stages in the Life of a Partnership
Partnerships don't just happen. They require strategic vision and practical, steady work.

Strategic partnerships go through at least three stages from the first idea to an effective force for the Kingdom. The three main stages are exploration, formation and operation.

Stage 1: Exploration
The exploration stage of effective partnership development is often the lonely work of a visionary.

The Value of Listening. Although you may have a vision, don't expect that everyone will or should automatically embrace it. The work depends upon building a common vision. Find out what others are doing. Get to know their histories, their visions, their problems and their needs. *The first task is listening!* And as you listen, also try to identify common objec-tives, or common needs that are shared by most of the potential partners.

Focus on building trust relationships. *Build good relationships person-*

ally with each of the potential partners. This will demonstrate respect for their work and a sincere interest in the life of the individuals.

Do not minimize the differences. Freely *acknowledge distinctives* of purpose, history, style, theology or philosophy among the ministries involved. By giving people the opportunity to be who they are, we can work with them in love, building toward functional unity. *Don't minimize differences, but do focus on common concerns.*

When you have identified a common concern worthy of a united effort, gently challenge potential partners to discover ways to meet those needs and objectives. Is it possible they might be more success-ful by working with others who face the same issues, and can offer different or additional resources?

The Value of Relationships. As you continue to visit and build rela-tionships, discussing partnership possibilities, be alert to the following:

- *Recognition of a common problem,* or need. This is an essen-tial starting point. Potential partners must identify with a limited, high-value, achievable objective that will give participants a sense of fulfillment and progress.
- *Recognition of benefits.* While you may join hands with others to reach and serve your community or city, each church must identify the benefits to its own congregation, beyond what it could accomplish by "going it alone."
- *Practical, tangible service* at the human level. This is essential if the partnership is to successfully serve peo-ple and give the participants a sense of fulfillment.
- *Agreement among pastors and leaders* of partner church-es. Each needs to understand and be sold on the con-cept of working together if a partnership is to thrive or even survive. The partnership needs a champion in every partner ministry.

Once the idea of working together begins to sprout in the thinking of sev-eral potential partner churches, you may be ready to call a first meeting.

Stage 2: Formation

The formation of a community or citywide strategic partnership usually occurs at or grows out of an initial meeting where all the players can meet, interact, pray and plan together. The following is a checklist to review before calling the first general meeting of the potential partnership:

1. The partnership facilitator personally knows the key leader(s) of each potential partner church or local ministry and something about his or her work and vision.
2. A common problem or need has been identified that potential partners feel is worth discussing and praying about together.
3. The potential partners are willing to at least *explore* coordinated efforts to meet the need.

Partnership Tip: Calling a formal meeting too early can kill the partnership!

First Meeting: Critical Launch Time for Partnership! At the end of your first meeting, you want the participants to feel:

- They were "heard" and their ideas were taken seriously. From that, they will have a sense of ownership.
- The meeting was conducted efficiently and smoothly while allowing all points of view to be aired in a reasonable way.
- That the issues being discussed were important and relevant to their lives—not trivial or theoretical.
- A sense of fulfillment: People will not let others waste their time. Because they have invested their time, they need to have a sense of accomplishment...even if the first action steps were modest.
- A sense of hope: Because of the spirit, vision and realistic objectives, a possibility exists that something of lasting value will be birthed through the cooperative effort.

Accomplish those objectives with the participants, and you will be well on your way toward an effective ministry partnership that could change your community, or even the whole city! To see that sort of meeting happen, the following are some specific suggestions:

Make sure people understand the purpose of the meeting. Having limited objectives for the meeting itself is important. The objectives have to be valuable—but limited.

Aim to set limited project goals in the beginning. Set limited, common objectives that can be met. Most pastors and leaders are too busy to just sit and talk at another meeting. They need to see real promise of progress, or they will not follow through and will not come back for many more meetings. Setting too ambitious a goal will probably cause failure. Partnerships have frequently failed because they attempted to accomplish the whole vision too soon, without clear plans and specific, small, "doable" steps—particularly in the beginning.

Define action steps. Clearly define the next steps. For projects, do enough initial planning so everyone knows who is responsible for developing or coordinating the next steps.

Set dates. Usually, dates should be set for upcoming meetings, and deadlines for the action steps. If the group is able to move along fast, several working groups may be established to develop or coordinate special areas or field projects. Create a plan for further communication among the group.

Cover administrative essentials. Cover the necessary administrative and financial issues. Make sure confidentiality guidelines, if necessary, are developed, understood and agreed upon. If there are to be joint projects, initiate plans for handling funds for the project. In some cases, joint fund-raising is helpful.

Agree on reporting. Make sure there is discussion and agreement about how the project will be reported. Who gets the credit? Partnerships usually encourage sharing the credit. What a remarkable idea!

Do not try to write a theology statement. Acknowledge differences, but focus on the common problem and what the cooperating ministries share in common. Forcing theological agreement focuses on differences, magnifying them. The need, the partnership and the biblical approach will self-select partners, especially in evangelism.

Worship together. God cares about us as sons and daughters, not just about the labor we represent for building His Church. Pray personally for each other, and, when possible, share communion with one another. Having humbled ourselves before God, it is easier to humble ourselves before each other.

Stage 3: Operational

A partnership facilitator is the key to success once you reach the operational stage. This person should be someone with vision and the ability to do the practical, day-to-day follow-through that is *essential* to get the partnership functioning and see it eventually bear real fruit. This may or may not be the same person who worked to initiate the partnership. The facilitator, then, needs to be working with everyone to:

1. *Secure and explain the benefits of partnership* to *each church*. Each participating ministry must see how the partnership helps it reach its goals. The participants must truly believe the partnership will be beneficial.
2. *Focus on relationships.* Maintain ongoing contact with all of the partners. Be supportive of their work and personal lives as well as their partnership roles. Encourage partners to stay connected, but recognize that the partnership facilitator may be the key link for a while.

Operation Tip: A survey of churches and ministry agencies that have tried some form of partnership revealed lack of communication as the number one problem.

The following books will be helpful resources:

Partners in the Gospel, (The Billy Graham Center, Wheaton College) and *Kingdom Partnerships for Synergy in Missions* (Carey Library, Pasadena).

For further information call or write:
Interdev, P.O. Box 30945
Seattle, WA 98103, U.S.A.
Telephone: (206) 775-8330
Fax: (206) 775-8326
E-mail: interdev-us@xc.org

THE NET—SERVING TOGETHER

BY JAAN HEINMETS

JAAN HEINMETS

Jaan Heinmets has been on staff with Campus Crusade since 1972 when he served as National Director of his native country, Sweden. He then ministered as a missionary to the Soviet Union for nearly 10 years. In 1983 he and his family became based out of Colorado Springs. Jaan has continued his training ministry to the Soviet Union, using the *JESUS* film as a vital evangelistic tool. In Colorado Springs he has coordinated numerous community-based projects, and was recently named president of THE NET— Serving Together.

A move of God's Spirit is occurring among the churches in Colorado Springs. Church leaders are putting aside their differences, and are working together to reach our city for Christ.

More than 60 churches have formally joined together to impact Colorado Springs with the love of Jesus. Now let's look at how this has come about.

During the past few years, pastors have been meeting biweekly for prayer through our local Association of Evangelicals. This prayer time has resulted in cohesive relationships and a spirit of love and trust among the spiritual leaders. They know that if problems or differences occur, they can go to each other. Because of the relationships established through pastors' prayer meetings, they now have a platform to deal with their differences.

These relationships are especially helpful when church members leave one church to join another. In the past, criticisms spoken by Christians about other churches were sometimes repeated by pastors. Now we do not tolerate this; instead, we try to deal with any negative talk. Pastors openly pray for each other in a supportive way during worship services, and their congregations are excited to see them praying for other churches and pastors.

UNITY: THE SPRINGBOARD FOR CITYWIDE EVANGELISM

When Greg Laurie came to Colorado Springs to conduct a Harvest Crusade (an evangelistic outreach much like Billy Graham's), the pastors already knew and trusted each other, thus, they were willing to work together.

They asked if I, as a staff member of Campus Crusade for Christ, would coordinate the crusade. The pastors felt comfortable having me do this, knowing I would balance my representation of various churches and their interests.

As a servant ministry worker (*In Colorado Springs we use the term "servant ministry" as a positive alternative to the term "parachurch ministry."*), they knew I would be able to represent the Church at large. It is important to note, however, that another reason I was asked and trusted with this responsibility is that I am active in my local church, Woodmen Valley Chapel. The pastors realized that as a servant ministry worker, I would be committed to the local churches. We had more than 130 churches join with us in the crusade.

An evaluation meeting took place after the crusade, and the pastors communicated a strong desire to continue working together to reach our city with the gospel. As a result, the pastors of the three largest congregations in Colorado Springs asked me to be a facilitator in uniting the churches of our city.

An organization was formed called "THE NET—Serving Together" and churches were asked to formally unite. We formed a

Declaration of Interdependence, which stated our purpose, our absolutes and our objectives.

OUR DECLARATION OF INTERDEPENDENCE

Our Purpose: We the churches in the Colorado Springs area want to work together in fulfilling the Great Commission. We will *utilize* our theological, cultural, denominational and traditional differences in working together to further the kingdom of God.

Our Absolutes: We believe the Bible is our sole source of authority for faith and practice. We believe in the person and works of Jesus Christ...
> Fully God,
> Fully Man,
> For full salvation as Lord and Savior.

Our Objectives: We want to...
> *Pray* Together,
> *Plan* Together,
> *Go* Together, and
> *Grow* Together.

CHURCHES IN DEED HELPING CHURCHES IN NEED

As THE NET, we have been able to become involved in helping to fight youth violence in our city, and we help feed the needy.

A few months ago, Calvin Johnson, a pastor whose church is in an area adversely affected by youth violence and gangs, contacted us to ask if we could bring the churches together to help address these problems. We contacted the churches, and together we held a prayer rally in the local high school.

We also came together to distribute the *JESUS* video in our community. One church could not afford a project of this magnitude; but when we joined together, we were able to purchase and distribute the video throughout the city. It was exciting and rewarding to see how the relationships among the churches were strengthened, and to see the pastors loving and respecting each other.

The following is a look at our present list of values:

The Whole Body Taking the Whole Gospel to the Whole Community

- There is only one Church of Colorado Springs, and it meets in many locations.
- Healthy churches desire to be growing churches.
- When one church prospers, the Body of Christ is strengthened. When one church suffers, we all suffer.
- Biblical unity is enhanced by embracing the diversity within the Body of Christ.
- The Church of Colorado Springs is strengthened when pastors and members affirm one another.
- The corporate witness of the Church is enhanced when churches love one another.
- The Body of Christ should continue to grow until everyone in Colorado Springs is given an opportunity to become a disciple of Christ.
- Servant ministries and missions agencies are valuable expressions within the Body of Christ, and churches are encouraged to partnership with them.

Jaan Heinmets can be reached at:
THE NET (Athletes in Action/Co-Mission office)
421 Woodmen Road
Colorado Springs, CO 80919
Phone: (719) 593-8200
Fax: (719) 593-8816

UTILIZING CULTURAL DISTINCTIVES

(COMPLEMENT OR CONFLICT)

BY TONY EVANS

TONY EVANS

Dr. Tony Evans is cofounder and senior pastor of the 3,000-member Oak Cliff Bible Fellowship in Dallas, Texas. He is also founder and president of The Urban Alternative. Dr. Evans's radio broadcast, "The Alternative with Dr. Tony Evans" can be heard on 250 stations daily in the United States and 40 countries worldwide. He is a widely acclaimed speaker for crusades and conferences throughout the world. Dr. Evans is the renowned author of 11 books, in addition to many other booklets, articles, newsletters and videos.

In Genesis 2:18, God said, "It is not good for the man to be alone. I will make him a helper suitable for him." The Hebrew word for "helper" suggests one who complements her husband so the two can become one. The idea is that as she, as helper, complements him, as head, the two would benefit from each other's different strengths, experiences, abilities, personalities and views of God in working together to accomplish the will of God for them in their family, church and community.

All Christians make up this one Body. As a wife to a husband, Christians must first work in unity to complement each other with their differences before the Church is to be used by God to help Him accomplish His will upon the earth.

Ephesians 6:22-31 speaks about the role of the husband and wife. But in verse 33 God explains that by using the illustration of the husband and wife, He is really talking about Christ and the Church. First Corinthians 10:17 also calls this Church one Body. And 1 Corinthians

WHEN PEOPLE ARE IN RELATIONSHIPS, THEY SEEK TO EMPOWER EACH OTHER AS THEY ARE COMMANDED TO SERVE ONE ANOTHER.

12:12 says: "For even as the body is one and yet has many members, and all the members of the body, though they are many, are one body" (*NASB*). Verse 25 tells us "that there should be no division in the body, but that the members should have the same care for one another" (*NASB*).

We have had plenty of sensitivity training and racial focus groups. While those things are important, the crisis we now face as a culture does not allow for theory without practice. "It's time for a change," the Winans sing. This is true, and the time is *now*. If not you, who? If not now, when?

Only by allowing the Bible to be the standard by which we judge ourselves and others can we experience the power necessary to be the kind of salt and light that can save a decaying society. The real issue is not about the temporary concerns of our society, but the fulfillment of an eternal plan. Each Christian has a job to do in helping to fulfill that plan.

WHERE TO START

First, in utilizing cultural differences, the key is starting where you are with who you know, and understanding that ministries develop out of relationships. Reconciliation that is predicated upon relationships has a greater chance of working than agendas based upon fear and guilt. Relationships build partnerships. The absence of relationships can lead to paternalism or inauthentic service.

When people are in relationships, they seek to empower each other as they are commanded to serve one another. As a result, they become greatly interested in utilizing cultural differences, because they receive joy by learning from or growing in the relationship. Those things that were the roots of anger or fear become points of discussion as they minister together, thus, they can minister with a better understanding of one another.

Second, ministering together cross-culturally has many of the same ingredients as ministering to someone from the same culture. Most have in common the same set of hopes, desires for a better home, church and community life. And most have similar struggles, because we all share a common venue of life. On the other hand, though some of society's concerns are universal, others seem somewhat more indigenous to particular groups of people. Therefore, as individuals minister together cross-culturally, a sincere agreement must be evidenced by their actions that all group's concerns are equally important and treated accordingly.

Third, we need to be open to learning from our differences. Although the essence of God never changes, it is amazing to note the many ways He has expressed Himself throughout history. The lives of Christians all around the world have been enriched from the testimonies of others about the greatness of God experienced in places like Africa, Asia, Europe, Central America and the Middle East. Hearing testimonies allows us to see Christ through our different ways of expression and communication. When people from different cultural backgrounds work side by side, they not only gain a testimony, but they also have the opportunity to learn from their differences. Our differences are a testimony to the creativity of God.

As a result, we should, in whatever legitimate ways possible, affirm the cultural distinctives of others as highly as we would our own. One example of this is the difference in worship styles. The creativity in dance, song, instruments, reading and so on invites us to see the creativity of the God who crafted the artistic designs of the universe. The uniqueness of the universe attests to His unique existence. Other false gods claim to be rulers; but outside of the god of evolution, none claim to have so artistically crafted the universe out of nothing.

And finally, we must eliminate stereotypes. This often means changing our own perspectives and perceptions about our differences. To do this as we work side by side, we have to talk through prejudices with the goal of decreasing the negatives and accentuating the positives. The amount of change we see depends on the amount of effort we invest. Above all, we need to remember that Christ says the greatest indicator of His lordship in our lives is the love we unconditionally show one another.

It is not easy for us to love this way, mainly because it is not natural to us—not only culturally, but also as redeemed sinners. Fighting to win over our sin natures requires an enabling power far greater than we can summon through our own inner strength. It requires a power that only total dependence upon the Holy Spirit can produce, and a power whose greatest goal is the glorification of Christ (see John 16:7-15).

For more information about The Urban Alternative, contact:

Dr. Anthony T. Evans
The Urban Alternative
P.O. Box 4000
Dallas, TX 75208
Phone: (214) 943-3868
Fax: (214) 943-2632

You Need Information

BY GEORGE BARNA

GEORGE BARNA

George Barna is president of the Barna Research Group, Ltd, a full-service marketing research company located in Oxnard, California. The company specializes in research for Christian churches and church-related groups. Among his clients have been the Billy Graham Evangelistic Association, Focus on the Family and World Vision. He has written more than 20 books (many best-sellers), and received several national awards. Barna is also the senior editor of *The Barna Report*, a bimonthly newsletter, and is the featured presenter in numerous video and audiotapes.

Some church leaders consider the process of incorporating information into their planning, and wonder why they should bother. Why not just *do our best and pray that it's blessed?*

If you arrive at this point, you may find yourself wrestling with a few of the following questions. (I have taken the liberty of answering those question on the basis of our past experience with corporate and church clients alike.)

Q. I am an expert in my field. Can't I simply operate on the basis of my experience and instinct?

A. Yes, you can, and many do. Some people are gifted with sharp instincts—but those instincts have been honed by exposure to the right information. This information, then, provides the keen insights that lead to what looks like effortless, intuitive decisions. This intuition, however, is invariably based on information gleaned in uncanny ways. Be aware that relatively few people have such abilities. The evidence suggests that success is a direct function of the accuracy and inspired use of targeted information.

Q. Why spend time and money to gather information? Can't I simply do my best and learn from my mistakes?

A. You certainly can...and you increase by more than tenfold the chances of running your organization out of business within five years! Trial and error, as this approach is commonly termed, is the most costly form of collecting and analyzing information. Often, the people who make the errors on which new insights are based are not in business long enough to benefit from their adventure in seat-of-the-pants marketing research.

Q. I am running a church, not IBM—how can we afford to buy information? Besides, this is not a for-profit company.

A. In actuality, you can't afford not to collect and analyze pertinent information about your ministry. Although many reasons exist for the large number of lethargic, inert churches in America, a key reason is that the principles in the ministry are not adequately attuned to the environment these churches are seeking to influence. These leaders mean well, but they are out of touch with the hearts and minds of the people they wish to change. Without that sensitivity, they have a severely reduced potential for creating ministry strategies that make a difference.

Whether you are running a for-profit or not-for-profit organization, you spend your hours on the job using God-given talents in His service. You should, therefore, make the best possible decisions and strive for the most efficient use of your resources. The value of information is that, when properly applied, it will enable you to make better decisions.

Q. Isn't it improper for a minister of the gospel to rely upon anything other than God for guidance?

A. Absolutely. But recognize that He provides guidance in myriad forms—including information that can be gathered and evaluated through your God-given talents and resources. He calls you to use the abilities and real-world information He has provided to arrive at logical, reasonable conclusions.

TYPICAL USES OF INFORMATION

The applications of information in the decision-making process are nearly infinite. From a church-marketing standpoint, I will present some of the most common applications. Think through the potential uses of information in your ministry before you create a plan to collect information. Some productive uses of such information for church ministry have included the following:

- Identify prime locations for a new church.
- Understand the background characteristics of the people within a ministry area.
- Predict the demographic changes in the community that will occur in the next few years, assuming that the current trends continue unabated.
- Describe the lifestyles and daily preferences of the people living in the community.
- Project expected church growth to prepare for the facilities, programming and personal needs of the future.
- Understand the background characteristics of the people who are currently in the congregation.
- Test new ideas or materials to be used for church marketing, outreach or fund-raising.
- Evaluate existing levels of awareness and image about your church, and the others in your community.
- Determine why some churches have achieved growth in your community while others have plateaued or declined.
- Identify the personal, felt needs of the people you will minister to.
- Determine the financial capacity of your church.

- Measure the impact of the church on people's lives.
- Evaluate the different elements of the church's ministry: preaching, teaching, worship, music, facilities, relationships, programs and so on.

Some of this information can be gathered through the acquisition and application of secondary data (information that has already been collected by someone else for their own purposes, but has been made available for your use); others almost always require you to conduct primary research (your own fact-finding mission to generate your own data). Perhaps those for which secondary data sources are most available and reliable are the first four items mentioned in the preceding list.

As you ponder your many options, you will realize that before you can determine exactly what information you need, you must grapple with a second basic question: Why do you need this information? One of the most important steps in the process is determining beforehand how you will use the information you think you need. Once you have identified the potential application, you are in a better position to evaluate the actual importance and value of the information.

The following books by George Barna are just a few of the powerful resources he has written:

The Frog in the Kettle, User Friendly Churches, The Power of Vision, Evangelism That Works and *Turning Vision into Action.*

For additional information about the Barna Research Group or available resources, write to:

Barna Research Group, Ltd.
2487 Ivory Way
Oxnard, CA 93030

SPIRITUAL MAPPING

BY GEORGE OTIS, JR.

GEORGE OTIS, JR.

George Otis, Jr., is founder and president of The Sentinel Group, a Seattle-based Christian research and information agency. He served as senior associate for the Restricted Access World with the Lausanne Committee for World Evangelism, and presently co-coordinates the United Prayer Track with Dr. C. Peter Wagner for the A.D. 2000 and Beyond Movement. George Otis, Jr., is the author of three books and is a well respected, internationally known speaker.

At first glance, the world we live in can appear to be a complex and bewildering place, a tangled web of borders and ideologies, agencies and revolutions. To help us sort it all out, we generally turn to cartographers (mappers), historians and, most of all, journalists. By putting their knowledge to work for us, we hope to make some sense of today's world. Yet, as Christians we have been taught by Scripture and tradition to acknowledge the spiritual dimension as the true nucleus of reality. Human endeavor is a related, but dependent outer layer.

Christian warriors at the end of the twentieth century can expect to face challenges on the spiritual battlefield that are unique in both type and magnitude. "Natural" methods of discerning and respond-

MISSION AGENCIES ARE REALIZING THAT CROSS-CULTURAL SAVVY ALONE CANNOT ACHIEVE EVANGELISTIC BREAKTHROUGHS.

ing to these challenges will no longer do. Local churches are discovering that church growth demographics do not tell us everything about our communities. Mission agencies are realizing that cross-cultural savvy alone cannot achieve evangelistic breakthroughs. Intercessory prayer fellowships are acknowledging the need for more specifically targeted coordinates. People want answers to the riddle of the invisible world so they can minister more effectively.

We are in an hour when the spiritual hosts of darkness are deploying for what may prove to be some of *the* most consequential battles of history. If we are to emerge from these spiritual encounters triumphantly, we must improve our ability to detect the true circumstances behind the headlines and to identify correctly authentic centers of power. In short, we must learn to see the world as it really is, not as it appears to be.

TERRITORIAL STRONGHOLDS

Nested near the heart of the spiritual mapping philosophy is the concept of territorial strongholds. Almost everyone has had the experience of entering another city, neighborhood or country only to sense an intangible unease or oppression descend upon their spirits. In Scripture, certain "spiritual strongmen" (high-ranking spirits) are referred to by the territories they control. These include the prince of Persia (see Dan. 10:13), the prince of Greece (see Dan. 10:20), the king of Tyre (see Ezek. 28:12) and the spirit of Babylon (see Rev. 17:3-5).

C. Peter Wagner, in his book *Wrestling with Dark Angels* (Regal

Books), suggests that Satan delegates high-ranking spirits to control nations, regions, cities, tribes, people groups, neighborhoods and other significant social networks. The major assignment of these demonic powers, Wagner believes, "is to prevent God from being glorified in their territory."[1]

ESTABLISHING TERRITORIAL STRONGHOLDS

If we are to understand why things are the way they are today, we must first examine what happened yesterday. Unfortunately, the overwhelming majority of people down through history have elected to exchange the revelations of God for a lie. In return for a particular deity's consent to resolve their immediate traumas, they have offered up their ongoing allegiance. It is through the placement of these ancient welcome mats that demonic and territorial strongholds are established.

Because many of the oldest pacts between peoples and demonic powers were transacted in Asia, and Asia now hosts the planet's greatest population center, it should not surprise us that the continent presently dominates the great unreached frontier known as the 10/40 Window. Population and pact longevity both have a great deal to do with the territorial entrenchment of spiritual darkness.

THE EXPANSION OF DARKNESS

One way territorial strongholds expand is through the broadcast of ideological or spiritual influence from transmission sites, or export centers, in various areas of the world. Examples of such centers include Cairo, Tripoli, Karbala, Qom and Mecca in the Muslim world; Allahabad and Varanasi in the Hindu world; Dharamsala and Tokyo in the Buddhist world; and Amsterdam, New York, Paris and Hollywood in the materialistic world.

Whereas the deflector shields of Judeo-Christian values once kept such poison from seeping too deeply into North America, the erosion of Christian commitment in recent years has unfortunately come to mean that, in an increasing number of instances, the enemy is now among us.

THE THRESHOLD GENERATION

Christian warriors who dare to march the final road toward world evangelization will face formidable opposition from an implacable and invisible adversary. If their mission to liberate enchanted prisoners is to succeed, they will require accurate intelligence on enemy command and control centers, and the spiritual equivalent of the military's night-vision goggles.

To do spiritual mapping in your city I recommend *Breaking Strongholds in Your City* by C. Peter Wagner (Regal Books) and *The Spiritual Mapping Field Guide* from my office.

For additional information about this subject, contact:
The Sentinel Group
P.O. Box 6334
Lynnwood, WA 98036
Phone: (206) 672-2989

AS WE WORK TOGETHER, REVIVAL WILL COME.

ARE WE READY?

BY JACK L. DENNISON

JACK L. DENNISON

Dr. Dennison is the North American regional coordinator for DAWN Ministries. For 7 years he served on the faculty of Multnomah Biblical Seminary's Pastoral Theology Department, teaching about church growth and related subjects. Dr. Dennison has been a United States Army Reserve Chaplain for 27 years and is a member of the Board of Directors for Project Amazon, a mission committed to planting 100,000 churches in the Amazon basin of Brazil.

There is a growing expectancy in our land that God is about to do something extraordinary—that we could be on the verge of a mighty awakening, leading to the evangelization of America.

The vision for the discipling of nations in our time that the Lord gave to Jim Montgomery, president of DAWN Ministries, is to "Fill the earth with the knowledge of the glory of the Lord." This will be accomplished by multiplying evangelical congregations until one is within easy access of every person in the world.

This has become known as the DAWN (Discipling A Whole Nation) strategy. It has now been embraced by top-level national leaders in more than 100 nations of the world and a growing number of cities in America with a total goal of almost 3 million more churches to be planted. Saturating the world with gatherings of believers is clearly the single most important factor leading directly to completing the Great Commission in our generation.

As Montgomery states, however, "Church planting in America is a hard sell. There is the feeling among pastors and denominational leaders that there are already enough struggling, half-full congregations as it is without starting more of the same kind."

But let me explain why I believe the DAWN vision of the need for at least 150,000 new congregations in America is consistent with what God has been saying to evangelical leaders throughout the world, and what He surely desires for our land as well.

First, we need more entry points into the Church for the new converts who come to Christ during a revival. Our current structure is unprepared for their influx.

The primary lesson of "the miracle of Modesto," was not that 35,000 people came to know the Lord in an eight-week period. Rather, it was the tragedy of its early demise. The church was so overwhelmed by the sheer number of people coming to Christ that they chose to discontinue the drama presentation God was using as the fuel behind the revival.

Bethany World Prayer Center in Baker, Louisiana, had a similar revival several years ago. During a 21-day period more than 18,000 people came to Christ. When Senior Pastor Larry Stockstill realized that his church and the neighboring churches combined could not assimilate the new believers, he launched what has become one of the most successful cell systems in America. He now believes that to maintain substantial harvest, more cells are needed. We at DAWN believe Larry is right; but that in many cities, the new cells are, in fact, new churches being planted.

The second reason we need an additional 150,000 new churches in America is because of the cultural distance that has grown between the Church and those coming to Christ today.

The cultural environment in the majority of our churches is so foreign, uncomfortable and uninviting to many new converts that it actually repels rather than attracts people to the Church. This church culture is so ingrained in the majority of our congregations that they simply will not change. It will therefore remain an impenetrable barrier for most new converts looking for a church home.

New wineskins are needed for the new wine of revival. Willowcreek near Chicago (14,000 members), Saddleback near Los Angeles (12,000 members) and First Assembly in Phoenix (14,000 members) are all examples of how a radically altered culture inside the local church was the invitation to massive evangelism and growth from outside the Church.

As the ethnic makeup of America continues to change, it is imperative that our church-outreach strategies and cultures change quickly enough to evangelize within our newfound diversity. We may soon need 150,000 new church plants in America to minister to ethnic niches alone.

More than 100 ethnic groups live in Portland, Oregon, most of which remain unreached or under-evangelized. The 100,000-member Hispanic community has only one percent of its population attending a Protestant church. Houston, Texas, alone has more Vietnamese than any whole state in the union, but one. There are 44,000 Filipinos in Las Vegas; 40,000 Hmong in Fresno; 34,000 Chinese in St. Louis. In the Dallas school system, a total of 94 different language groups are represented. Currently, according to researcher George Barna, 32 million people in America speak some language other than English as their primary language.

The inner city of America has become home to a countless number of ethnic groups, including a large percentage of the nation's black, Hispanic and other major ethnic populations. What can be said of the Church's effectiveness in reaching these people living in these places?

The simple conclusion from these factors is that we need tens of thousands more churches if we are going to provide a church for every person in every ethnic, geographic, cultural and sociological grouping of people in America.

For this task, each city in America needs to have a comprehensive plan, that if successful, would lead directly to the discipling of the whole city. And this can only be done by filling every piece of its cultural mosaic with vibrant cells of believers incarnating the life of our Lord Jesus Christ and proclaiming His message.

Much of what God wants to do in ministering to the cities of

America cannot be fully accomplished while millions of Americans live beyond the reach of His Son, separated by ethnicity, geography or culture. It is the responsibility of the Church to ensure that every person in our nation is within access of a gathering of believers with whom they can identify ethnically, and culturally. We are currently a long way from this reality.

As we plant these 150,000 new churches in our nation, skyrocketing land costs as well as zoning laws are becoming more and more restrictive. We will be forced therefore to diversify from the facility-based church ministries that are common in America today. In order to promote the growth of the Church in the midst of these obstacles, we will have to broaden our definition of "church" and legitimize new models. Throughout the next few years, we will learn more about multi-congregational churches, satellite churches, cell-churches and networks of house churches.

Out of this process will emerge, over time, a clear and comprehensive plan that will give God's "prophetic call and message" to the Church regarding what He wants to do in the city and how He wants to do it. This message and plan will form the basis for the Church's organic unity to become functional as we pursue the common destination together, a destination of filling the cities of America with the presence of Christ.

Note
1. C. Peter Wagner, *Wrestling with Dark Angels* (Ventura, CA: Regal Books, 1990), p. 77.

For the full story of DAWN, read Jim Montgomery's *DAWN 2000: 7 Million Churches to Go* and his follow-up book.

To obtain further information contact:
DAWN Ministries
7889 Lexington
Colorado Springs, CO 80920
Phone: (719) 548-7460
Fax: (719) 548-7475

GO TOGETHER

WE CAN ONLY ACCOMPLISH THIS TOGETHER
BY TED HAGGARD

As we prepare to implement the strategies the Lord has provided for our communities, we are compelled to ask some of the hard questions:

- I already have so much to do, why should I do this as well?
- This does sound exciting, but I was excited about the last book I read, too. I like the idea, but I don't want to find myself disappointed by trying, and then failing, at motivating other leaders in my city. Why should I make myself vulnerable by attempting to persuade them to work together?

I am sympathetic to these questions. I, too, pastor a church and have a family that, combined, requires more hours than are available in any day. But several years ago I had two experiences that permanently altered the focus of my time.

Shortly after completing college, I worked with World Missions for Jesus, a (West) German missions organization that served the suffering Church behind the Iron Curtain, as well as those in socialistic countries. Regularly we assisted families whose Christian fathers had mysteriously disappeared, or parents whose Christian sons were missing because of government persecution. People within our mission frequently risked their lives smuggling Bibles in to their less fortunate sisters and brothers in Christ. We helped believers whose churches had been destroyed (often while occupied).

We were oblivious to the denominational affiliation of suffering believers—Baptists or Pentecostals—it did not matter. We only knew

TIME IS A GIFT GOD HAS GIVEN US TO SERVE THE MOST PEOPLE POSSIBLE.

and cared that they were people who were grateful to the Lord Jesus and in need of love from Christ's Body in the West.

We were also aware of the overall strength of the Body of Christ in each region. If believers had become fragmented and separated from one another, we knew it would be just a matter of time before they became unnecessarily vulnerable to the anti-Christ forces determined to eliminate them.

My worldview was also molded during a night in 1980, when I sat on the platform at Dr. Cho's church in Seoul, South Korea. My Bible had fallen open to 2 Corinthians 5:11 where Paul wrote, "Knowing therefore the terror of the Lord, we persuade men" (*KJV*). Then in a split second I saw burning people: screaming, gasping and groping for relief. They were clawing and desperately searching for a breath of clean air...babies, children, teens and adults—their skin bubbling on fire—forever.

I did not know if I had seen a split-second vision, or had just imagined something; but I knew that whatever the suffering of hell must be like, the atrocities of earth did not compare. And this terror did not seem to have any distinction among its people groups. Everyone was suffering—unnecessarily paying the price for their own sinfulness.

So in my mind, when we talk about the Church functioning as one Body to more effectively serve the lost with the gospel message, there is no room for debate. Time is a gift God has given us to serve the most people possible. We cannot afford to be prodigal with that gift; therefore this chapter and its accompanying Resources chapter (7) will provide some models of His strategies for reaching the lost. As Christian soldiers, we have no choice: We are commissioned to do so! This is all we do. This is our purpose: making it hard to go to hell from our cities.

LEADERSHIP MEETINGS THAT WORK

Calvary Chapel Pastor Brent Spalding stood in front of 73 other senior pastors from the valley area, calling their attention to the charts on the wall behind him that pinpointed the local high schools and colleges. "Whose church will pray for Madison High School?" Marion from the Congregational Church lifted his hand. "And who wants Harrison High?" Steve indicated his church would target Harrison. As the afternoon meeting continued, every school, government building, major business, medical facility and church was assigned to the various pastors for a three-month saturation with prayer.

Then Brent pointed to a city map that had been marked by the 73 pastors as they arrived. Carter Torrey, a Methodist, outlined the areas surrounding these churches so each congregation would know which streets they were responsible to prayerwalk during the following three months. As pastors discussed their plans to pray over maps, neighborhoods and the public facilities they had just been assigned, differences evaporated in an atmosphere of common purpose: preparing the people of their city for the gospel.

In closing, Brent asked for three volunteers who would be willing to get together to study the information that had been collected by DAWN Ministries about the valley, so it could be presented at the following meeting. He held up the packet of research materials available for determining who to target in the city. Their task now as a group of churches would be to identify and target the various people groups within the city for evangelism. Donald Plush, a charismatic; Charles Harris from the Church of God in Christ; and Pastor Jeff Moreland from the Wesleyan Church agreed to coordinate the next meeting.

THREE MONTHS LATER

Ninety-seven senior pastors came to the fall meeting where one-year assignments of people groups were to be discussed. As the pastors gathered, a roar of discussion and laughter resonated. Small groups of pastors stood together drinking juice and munching on snacks while discussing their families, churches and their recently completed prayer emphasis.

Others perused the new charts. Some of those charts included current solid statistical data such as:

- Sixty-three percent of the population believes Jesus is the Son of God, and that the Bible at least includes the Word of God.
- Four percent of church attendees shared the gospel with someone in the last month.
- Sixty-nine percent of people in the valley could not accurately define a true Christian.

Some charts entitled Guesstimates revealed simple estimates from general observations in the community and from the newspaper. For example:

- Twenty percent of the community's churches were life-giving.
- Seven percent of the population attended a life-giving church on an average Sunday morning.

Other interesting charts included information about three prototype churches that were effective at winning and discipling non-Christian people. Below the charts were handouts explaining why these churches were being successful. The church charts also provided a representation of the 10 largest churches in the community. They too, were equipped with handouts that explored facts and possible reasons for their remarkable growth.

A large map drew the attention of some pastors. It marked:

- Churches;
- Bars;
- Occult activity sites;
- Government buildings;
- Prisons, jails, etc.;
- Income levels for neighborhoods;
- Crime rates for neighborhoods;
- Home owners in contrast to renters;
- Schools;
- New age book shops/activity centers;
- Unitarian and pagan places of worship;
- The Freemasons;
- Metropolitan community churches;
- Satanic sacrifice sites;
- Hospitals, with special markers for those with psychiatric wards;
- Abortion centers.

Donald Plush called the meeting to order by welcoming the new pastors to the valley. He then led the group in praying for and blessing those who were attending for the first time. When the prayer ended, the pastors again directed their attention to Donald.

Pastor Brad Gillispie, a Baptist, had only been in town two weeks. Brad could tell this was not an average ministerial group. He realized this group of pastors had obviously come to the meeting with an intentional focus and a unified purpose. His curiosity was heightened as Donald began delineating some specific charts prepared for that meeting.

Behind Donald was a series of charts listing groupings of people: social, occupational and ethnic.

- Social categories included college students, single parents, low-income families, veterans and various age groupings.
- The occupational charts seemed the most extensive,

with broad groupings such as health professionals, city government employees, real estate and food distribution. Under health professionals were groupings such as doctors, nurses and medical technicians. The chart diagramming city government employees started with the mayor and city council, and listed the various levels of employment that people have with the city. The real estate list consisted of developers, agents and government inspectors. Under food distribution were truck drivers, grocery store owners and check-out clerks.

- The ethnic chart included percentages for every people group represented in the valley's population.

After a short discussion, the pastors decided it would be wise to target the community using social systems and occupations rather than ethnic groupings. Some in the group believed that if the city were more segregated, ethnic strategies would be important. But because the valley was integrated, and people tend to be grouped according to profession and recreation, these two classifications would reach everyone.

Then the work began. Once the classifications were reduced to 97 (the number of senior pastors present), Donald asked Pastor Harris to explain the guidelines that would ensure their goal of "communicating the gospel, in an understandable way, to everyone within our population twice a year."

GUIDELINES

1. Every people group will have at least three churches responsible to pray, plan and implement a ministry to their target group.
2. The three churches targeting a group are encouraged to meet together to brainstorm about effective outreaches within their own resources and spheres of influence. They are to be the "dream team" to ensure that their group of people have an opportunity for ministry. Then, each church is expected to creatively develop independent methods of ministering to people within their target group.

3. Assignments are not exclusive. They do not imply "ownership" of a group or ministry. Instead, they are an attempt to distribute (share, focus and streamline) responsibility.
4. These target groups are for the purpose of strategically reaching into segments of the non-Christian community—not members of our target group who are within the Church. The purpose of these assignments has nothing to do with ministering to people within the group that are already Christians, but rather to reach unchurched members of the group.

Pastor Harris explained that through these assignments, we hoped to target our resources, strategically focusing our prayer abilities and creativity to develop intentional ministries to serve specific groups of people. He explained the reasoning for this approach: The group had observed that when all the churches tried to reach all the people, their resources were so diluted, they didn't reach any group of people well. In other words, no single church could be all things to all people.

After Pastor Harris answered the final guidelines question, Donald encouraged the groups of three to contact each other by conference call on a monthly basis. This call would facilitate their ability to maintain unity, update one another as new plans developed and pray together. He encouraged them to exchange E-mail and fax addresses, so they could send FYI memos regularly. He then announced that there would not be another meeting for four months when everyone would gather with their congregations for the March for Jesus downtown.

Then Donald gave everyone a choice for one of the two Steve Sjögren books: *Conspiracy of Kindness* or *Servant Warfare*. He explained that both of the books would give them creative ideas for reaching into the community. He laughingly told some stories from the books and, as the men chuckled, each gratefully received a book.

The atmosphere was so relaxed that the pastors acted as if they had nowhere else to go. They had found great value in being together.

When the meeting dismissed, everyone was talkative. They discussed the benefits they had experienced since they began purposefully focusing their ministries. Brad Gillispie, the new pastor, was

amazed. He had heard that the churches of the city had been growing steadily for the last few years through new converts, and he could
see the optimism among the pastors—but he still wondered:

*Why weren't pastors threatened by others getting a "better people
group" to target? Why weren't they jealous of the leaders? These men*

THE PASTORS REALIZED THEY WERE ABLE TO ACCOMPLISH MUCH MORE TOGETHER THAN THEY EVER COULD HAVE ALONE.

*seemed to genuinely like each other. No one was having to be cautiously gra-
cious, but rather they were relaxed and open....No suspicion or hesitation,
just relaxed optimism. How could this be?*

As Brad stood there thinking, Howard Farrell, the Christian
Reformed pastor, approached him with a personal welcome. Brad
immediately asked, "How did this begin? What is the history of this
group?"

Howard laughed and invited Brad to sit down. He explained that
this particular method of working together was relatively new, and
that it was the most effective communitywide effort they had ever
experienced. He attributed its genesis to years ago when the local
chapter of the National Association of Evangelicals (NAE) worked to
build mutual respect among the evangelical groups within the city.
He went on to say that when they published the Evangelical
Manifesto, they agreed to work together until they had achieved
"societal change" (note Don Argue's article in chapter 7). From those
decisions came the foundation for several additional efforts in the
city that even further galvanized the pastors.

Howard explained how annual Jesus Marches and the door-to-door
distribution of the *JESUS* video to every home in the city had created
a spiritual synergy. As a result, the pastors realized they were able to
accomplish much more together than they ever could have alone. And,
he said, they recognized their need for working together—it would

actually make work easier and more effective for all of them. They used the foundation of the Association of Evangelicals and the assistance of Mission America to form a broad-based group to coordinate their efforts, so everyone in their city would have an opportunity to respond to the gospel.

Since that time, Howard related, Mission America has continued to provide them with fresh ideas and the resources necessary to keep them focused on their city as a whole. He said materials from Impact Productions, Ed Silvoso, Peter Wagner, Bill Bright and Steve Sjögren had been particularly helpful. The Scriptures Howard referred to about the strength of the Body of Christ working harmoniously as one Body (see 1 Cor. 12; John 17) suddenly came alive in Brad. He understood: The Church works when it works together!

The room emptied. As they too were leaving, Howard paused to invite Brad to dinner with their wives so they could continue their conversation. Brad said he wanted to read Sjögren's book first, believing they would have more to discuss if he did. They arranged to get together in two weeks.

Two weeks later Brad was obviously excited about having dinner with Howard and his wife. They greeted each other warmly and introduced their wives; the conversation was effervescent. As a Baptist, Brad was delighted with the creativity of the Sjögren book and wanted to talk about it. Howard attempted to include the ladies in the conversation, but Brad's enthusiasm overwhelmed all other talk.

"I've been around evangelicals all of my life, but I've never heard of evangelism like this," Brad cheerfully announced, referring to Sjögren's book and the application of it he had witnessed in the valley. He started telling stories from the book, reciting ways they had influenced his view of evangelism within the secular community. Then he said that he had contacted Impact Productions in Tulsa to improve his church's media outreach into the community. He had also started formulating plans to help his church in the words of Sjögren "show the love of Jesus in a practical way."

Brad's enthusiasm continued to dominate the table, telling of his new view of ministry since arriving in the valley. When the others placed their food orders, Brad chose to ditto Howard's order because he didn't want to stop talking. Then, as the waiter served the food, Brad's enthusiasm subsided and he asked Howard, "How did these pastors get this way? How can I learn to think like this?"

Howard gently smiled and said that the thinking behind their consortium of churches began to work just after the death of Reverend Karl Lupton, the senior pastor of First Presbyterian Church who had served there for 27 years prior to his death. When he died, Howard recalled, his widow found a letter that he had written to be given to the other pastors in the community. That letter communicated the values that have provided the spiritual framework for the participants. Howard offered to send a copy of the letter to Brad.

OLD-FASHIONED WISDOM

Three days later Brad received a copy of Reverend Lupton's letter. It said:

My dear Fellow Pastors,

By the time you read this, I will be in the presence of our Lord. Just to have served with you these past years has been a distinct privilege, and I believe you are in a unique position to greatly influence the character of His Body as you enter the new millennium. It is my prayer that the twenty-first-century Church will not face the division and heartbreak those of us who served in the twentieth century endured.

In my later years of ministry, as I watched the transformation of our valley, I came to understand that few (maybe only one) reasons exist for division within the Body of Christ. Some Christian leaders try to find points of contention, but I have concluded they can't contribute to God's purpose. In our valley, however, many pastors do contribute greatly. You are among them.

In this final letter, I would like to mention some of the character traits you have exhibited that mark you as leaders who will set the stage for the Church in the twenty-first century.

1. Gratefulness. Because you maintain a grateful spirit, you don't threaten people or communicate a harsh gospel. Throughout my years, I have experienced nothing that opens as many doors as gratefulness.

2. Laughter. You laugh easily. If I could change anything in my ministry, this would be it—laugh more. You seem to have discovered the secret of maintaining an innocence, enabling you to laugh freely at yourselves and others.

3. Action. I have noticed that you take action on facts. It's easy to be misled by family tradition, personal comfort or emotional response. You, however, seem willing to make decisions and focus your ministries on the facts, such as heaven, hell, the Word of God, redemption and the society you must influence. Because you let facts motivate you, I believe you will be more useful than my generation.

4. Humility. This is so appealing. You are not uncomfortable when people don't know you, or mispronounce your name, or ignore you or simply aren't interested in your thoughts. You have unlimited freedom because of your humility. You don't appear to object to doing things someone else's way, which enables you to cooperate with someone else's vision. You understand teamwork, the family, the Body. In my view, you embrace sacrifice rather than demand your own opinions and methods. According to the Bible, "God resists the proud, but gives grace to the humble." Therefore, because of your humility, God can use you.

5. Spiritual Authority. You understand this principle. Absence of jealousy, along with freedom to accept your God-given role is liberating. You don't seem fearful of speaking out with freedom. But instead of demanding to be heard, you earn that right through your lives and ministries. Although I don't fully understand your eagerness to embrace change *by prayer and fasting, I believe you are asking God to use you in greater ways—which He is doing.*

6. Spirituality. You are not afraid of being spiritual. My generation was embarrassed to appear more spiritual than intellectual. You have balanced that. I appreciate your thoughtful submission to the Spirit, which allows you to speak freely about angels, demons, the Holy Spirit and the miraculous without falling into fanaticism.

I wish to express my deep appreciation for what I have seen and experienced while working with you. My generation knew too few of such simple characteristics. But because of these virtues, you will enjoy impacting the next century. Congratulations.

Perhaps I will look down as one of the cloud of witnesses and be able to cheer you on in your worldwide task.

May God bless you,
Reverend Karl Lupton

Now Brad understood! After reading the letter that had influenced the pastors in the valley so greatly, it seemed reasonable that the Christian leaders would commit themselves as one group to "going into all the(ir) world and preaching the gospel." It was clear, the Great Commission was the basis for all they were doing. As Brad thought, he realized he was actually working among men who understood the first-century Church, and were preparing to be a model twenty-first-century Church.

The letter had served as a catalyst for change. Brad decided he didn't have too much to do after all. Leading his church in fulfilling the Great Commission was all he had to do. And he understood that as he did this, the church he served would benefit more than he ever anticipated.

We are called to be God's agents for change in a world that is resistant to change. And we *can* do this by praying, planning and going together. Only together can we fulfill His great commission. Chapter 7 gives us more examples of how we can GO TOGETHER.

7

RESOURCES FOR "GOING TOGETHER"

IMPLEMENTING CITYWIDE STRATEGIES

CONTRIBUTORS:
PAUL CEDAR
JOHN QUAM
STEVE SJÖGREN
RUTH ANN MARTINEZ
LLOYD OLSON
TOM PELTON
DON ARGUE
TOM NEWMAN
ALICE SMITH

Implementing a strategy can be awkward in any community. This chapter provides resources written by nine outstanding leaders in implementation—they are all practitioners.

Each of these renowned leaders has helped to break down the barriers of bitterness and mistrust associated with citywide evangelization. Each offers effective, proven tools for serving, unifying and equipping the Body of Christ. Each aptly articulates the Supernatural dynamic that happens when leaders work together to love their cities into the Kingdom.

ONE SPIRIT, ONE BODY: SPIRITUAL SYNERGY

BY PAUL CEDAR AND JOHN QUAM

PAUL CEDAR   JOHN QUAM

Dr. Paul Cedar is an author, pastor and church leader, and serves as chairman and CEO of Mission America. He is also chairman of the International Coalition of the A.D. 2000 and Beyond Movement, and a guest dean at the Billy Graham Schools of Evangelism. Dr. Cedar serves on the advisory board of many Christian organizations. He has been named to *Who's Who in Religion*, *Who's Who in America* and *Who's Who in the World*. He and his wife, Jeanie, have three grown children.

John Quam and his wife, Carolyn, ministered for 10 years in Brazil as missionaries with OC International. John also served for 7 years with ACMC as Upper Midwest region-al director, and for 5 years as executive director of Concerts of Prayer International. John is currently national facilitator of City/Community Ministries for Mission America. He and his wife, Carolyn, have two married daughters.

"From him the whole body, joined and held together by every supporting ligament, grows and builds itself up in love, as each part does its work" (Eph. 4:16).

At a recent banquet in Minneapolis, an African-American pastor shared his heart and vision for his part of the city. Crime, poverty and various expressions of evil were overwhelming his neighborhood and taxing the ability of his church to minister effectively. As a part of a larger group of pastors and Christian leaders, he shared his concern and God led several suburban and urban pastors to join forces with him. As a result, a new ministry called Urban Hope was born. The banquet was a celebration of this new partnership and an expression of ongoing commitment to its success.

American cities are growing daily with a steady flow of diverse peoples. As they expand numerically and ethnically, they represent larger groupings of people, and therefore, a larger incidence of diversity. We experience this diversity in the Church by varying forms of worship, different theological convictions and contrasting approaches to ministry. God intended that our differences would make us more effective as His Body in a given community.

Fingers, hands, arms, legs and feet, each linked together, building up the whole Body, "in love." While this is God's intention, Satan's strategy is just the opposite. He wants to keep us divided, and even competing with each other.

When we read a verse in the New Testament about the Church, our first inclination is to apply that verse exclusively to our local congregations. This initial response is based on our church culture and training. We rarely think of those instructions for the whole Church in a given city. Instead of substituting the Church in Denver or Portland for the Church in Ephesus, we automatically think of our Faith Presbyterian or Grace Baptist Church where we serve or worship. How different our interpretations of the Bible and even our church practices would be if we saw first the whole Church in the whole city.

BUILDING UNITY THROUGH PRAYER

The ministry of prayer serves as a prime example: Most local churches spend time in their worship services praying for their own programs, leaders, plans, etc. Not many churches pray also for the church across the street, or the others in their neighborhoods and throughout the city, independent of their denominations or worship styles.

What if each church began to pray for other churches in their community, and from time to time gathered for united prayer services? What if pastors met regularly for prayer, or if once a year the pastors went away for a prayer retreat? How would this change the way the Church is viewed in the city? Would it not add to the credibility of the Christian message?

In addition, local congregations and other Christian ministries can be competitive. Christian ministries spring up frequently because the existing church, or an existing agency, is not doing an adequate job of meeting a special need. Sometimes a person leaves an existing ministry to start a new one.

At best there is a competition for financial resources and "market share." At worst there may be bitterness and competition. Mailing lists, for example, are often protected and donor bases are generally not shared with anyone. But what if the Christian Church in a given city or community decided to work together and made that information available to all Christian groups? What if they targeted unreached or poorly reached cultural groups and identified cooperative ways to present the gospel to each one using their diversity as a means to effectiveness rather than a reason for separation? Is this an appropriate way to apply Ephesians 4:16?

We are happy to report that examples of these kinds of "spiritual synergy" are emerging in exciting ways around the country. In Portland, for example, pastors began meeting together in prayer. Eventually they also brought their congregations together for a city-wide prayer event. Local churches purchased a full-page ad in the newspaper, listing the names of all the churches in the background, and in bold type declaring: "One Church, Many Congregations."

In Jackson, Mississippi, racial separation was prohibiting the Church from effectively demonstrating the love of Christ. A black evangelist and a white evangelist began working together, and

Mission Mississippi was born. Cooperative activities were planned, including lunches in the park with united worship and evangelism services. God is breaking down the walls in Jackson, Mississippi, and that vision is beginning to spread to other cities throughout the state.

As was mentioned in the first paragraph, Christian leaders have been meeting together in the Twin Cities of Minneapolis and Saint Paul. They have been praying and sharing their visions of bringing Christ's love to everyone in the area. One group is working on establishing neighborhood houses of prayer for every community; another is gathering needed statistical information.

Cooperative evangelistic efforts such as the Promise Keepers rallies at the Metrodome and the 1996 Billy Graham Crusade at the same site have provided additional networks for men, women, youth, children, etc. Pastoral prayer groups are meeting regularly in 19 regions throughout the metropolitan area. In addition, the Minnesota Prayer Coalition helps unite the leadership of many prayer ministries in a cooperative effort to expand the work of prayer in the Church.

These examples represent only a few of the citywide cooperation efforts that have been reported to us.

CELEBRATING OUR DIFFERENCES

We are convinced that the Church needs to rethink its approach to ministry in all cities and communities. Our differences are not reasons to separate us, but rather the gift of God to make us more effective in the larger community. Several years ago Ray Stedmen, who pastored the Peninsula Bible Church in California, wrote a book entitled *Body Life*. He emphasized the diversity of the gifts within the unity of the Body, and referred often to the Ephesians 4 passage.

Many have since written, taught and even expanded on this significant biblical concept. Most, however, have seen only the application to the local congregation. *They have missed the context of the city, which appears to us to be the primary contextual application of this passage because the book was written to the Church at Ephesus.*

The secular world has learned many lessons about business synergy. Today, a particular make of automobiles or trucks may actually have key parts made by one of its competitors. Restaurants or electronics stores will build right next to each other to create a particular kind of shopping zone. Working together leaves more energy for creativity rather than cutthroat competition.

Positioning for the future brings more results than protecting the past. Of course, for the Church, this means operating within the biblical framework that defines who we are and what the governing

POSITIONING FOR THE FUTURE BRINGS MORE RESULTS THAN PROTECTING THE PAST.

guidelines are for us and our corporate expressions. We must continually seek to understand scriptural truth and obey it.

The words of Jesus and the writings of Paul clearly exhort us to seek unity around our common purpose, show our love for one another and even prefer one another. Cooperative citywide vision is encouraged by the Scriptures and increases the effectiveness of the Church. Our hope is that thousands of cities and communities all across our nation will come together in cooperative vision for the work of the gospel.

While Satan has built spiritual strongholds in our thinking that resist the thought of broad, loving cooperation—Jesus prayed for it. So must we!

For further information, contact:
Mission America
901 East 78th Street
Minneapolis, MN 55420
Phone: (612) 853-1762
Fax: (612) 853-1745

SERVANT EVANGELISM, KINDNESS CAMPAIGNS

BY STEVE SJÖGREN

STEVE SJÖGREN

Steve Sjögren is the founding pastor of Vineyard Community Church in Cincinnati, Ohio, a 3,500-member church that has emphasized church planting, evangelism and care for the poor. He formerly planted churches in Oslo, Norway and Baltimore. Steve's books *Conspiracy of Kindness* (Vine Books) and *Servant Warfare* (Vine Books) have presented effective new approaches to sharing the love of Christ. He has served as the Association of Vineyard Churches regional director in the Ohio Valley, the head of the Vineyard's National Evangelism Task Force and associate editor of *Equipping the Saints* magazine.

DOING SMALL THINGS WITH GREAT LOVE TO REACH A CITY

In the early 1980s I was involved with the beginning of what became the Vineyard movement. The congregation where I was on staff was young, but dynamic. Within just two years this group had grown to over 2,000 with mostly unchurched people. When I left there and began to plant churches, I believed growth of that sort was normal. After inviting about 1,200 people, I was severely disappointed by our first service numbers—just 37 brave souls met in a barn used for square-dancing.

On the Monday following that unenthusiastic launch, I told the Lord, "You didn't send me here to touch a neighborhood. You put the desire in me to reach this city. Show me how to do this Your way."

Throughout the next few weeks the Lord began to redefine my strategy as a church planter. We had been broadcasting the message, "Come in," and were obviously not attracting the attention of many. Our new approach was exactly the opposite. We began to challenge our cozy group with the "go out" message.

I led as we began to serve in hundreds of creative ways—all for free, showing the city God's love in action. We had an absolutely free car wash with a big banner that announced, "Free Car Wash—No Donations Accepted!" Dozens came in, most not believing it really was for free. Later we began to feed parking meters, leaving a card that read, "Your parking meter looked hungry, so we fed it!" We also began to give away soft drinks with a card that read, "You looked too thirsty to pass up...." Sometimes we had short conversations; sometimes no words were exchanged.

Several powerful forces began to be unleashed as we carried out our serving projects. First, we were being directed outwardly. After our first car wash, about two dozen of us stood in a prayer circle and started to weep. We realized we had just talked to more non-Christians in the past couple of hours than we had in several previous years combined.

Second, those we served began to get a clear and positive impression of Christ and His Church. We weren't fund-raising, and we weren't coming across as parental figures trying to make them behave. Our sole reason for serving was to show them the love of Christ. Once they saw our hearts, they began to open theirs to us.

Before long, I was so focused on simply loving and serving people in practical ways, my role began to quietly be redefined. Without noticing the transformation, I almost forgot that I was a pastor. As I began to model servant evangelism for my congregation, my focus changed from inviting to serving. It virtually slipped my mind that I came here to start a new church!

Throughout the years we have experimented with approximately 150 creative ways of showing the love of Christ through practical application. Our service has resulted in a handful of lessons about sharing evangelism in a Christian culture that has become discouraged with evangelism.

EVANGELISM IS DOABLE

I call it "low risk—high grace." By making the focal point an act of service in the name of Christ, the challenge is significantly lowered: The average follower of Christ can participate. Though the act of service is a "no brainer," we do this with great dependence upon the Holy Spirit to make deep impressions on the people we serve. As we serve, we tell those we touch, "This is free to show you God's love in a practical way." That simple phrase captures both ends of the equation. It's simple and free. Anyone with a heart to serve can do this. But there is also something deeply spiritual going on when we serve in this way.

Some who have never tried to reach out with servant evangelism naturally wonder, *What good is it to give people a soft drink? That's something even non-Christians can do all the time.*

I'm not sure that sort of kindness is common in our day. (I can't remember the last time I was offered a free soft drink!) Humanitarians do exist in our age, but our kindness is very different from theirs. When Christians show the love of God with the Holy Spirit's power motivating them, something spiritual happens. Those we serve contact what Paul calls the "kindness of God." When that kindness is shown to people, results are inevitable: "the kindness of God leads you to repentance" (Rom. 2:4, *NASB*).

Last year my congregation of 3,500 touched about 18,000 in our city, doing servant evangelism projects. In the words of one evangelism veteran, "Son, that's a whole lot of God's love."

Evangelism Is a *Process*

None of us come to Christ in an instant. Paul told the Corinthians "I planted the seed, Apollos watered it, but God made it grow" (1 Cor. 3:6). We may pray to "close the deal" and place our faith in Christ, but the lion's share of the work of evangelism takes place in the quiet recesses of our hearts long before we are cognizant of what is going on.

The act of coming to Christ is always at least a bit mysterious. Even C.S. Lewis could not explain his own conversion precisely. His account was, "All I can tell you is when I got on the back of my brother's motorcycle, I didn't know Christ. When I got off at the London Zoo, I did know Him."

Based upon the truth of 2 Peter 3:9 (God is "not wanting anyone to perish, but everyone to come to repentance"), our job isn't necessarily to lead everyone in a sinner's prayer, but to help in escorting them to a place of readiness to eventually be able to pray that prayer.

Evangelism Is Connected with *Acceptance*

Once we have touched people with small acts of love, they will naturally become curious about our churches, and begin to gravitate toward them. When the unchurched community starts to show up in large numbers, another challenge becomes clear: speaking in a way they can comprehend.

We recently performed a discount gasoline outreach. When the price of gas jumped dramatically, we made arrangements with a station manager to pump gas, clean windshields and lower the price to just 99 cents for a couple of hours. We served hundreds of families, shared the love of Christ, caused a bit of a traffic jam and made a significant impression on many.

The manager was so excited that he went from car to car explaining, in his own words, what we were doing: "We're showing the love of God in a practical way!" To my knowledge he is not yet a "we"! But he felt the atmosphere of love and forgiveness present that day, and longed to be included among us.

Evangelism too often begins with an attitude of "ready, fire, aim." It seems to me, we have spent an enormous amount of time talking about changing the world, but little time actually doing much to bring about change. By redefining the beginning point of evangelism from speaking to showing God's love to the world, it's easy to launch out. As we serve the unchurched in small ways, with God's hand upon our lives, they will ask, "Tell me, why are you doing this?" No matter how strong our evangelism gifts, any Christian can answer the question.

Steve has authored several books, including *Servant Warfare* and *Conspiracy of Kindness* (both are Vine Books, Servant Publications, Ann Arbor, Michigan). For a more thorough explanation of servant evangelism, either of these books are excellent resources. His website has recent innovations and discoveries about serving our cities into relationships with Christ. That site is located at: http//www.kindness.com

NEED: THE UNITY FACTOR IN MONTERREY, MEXICO

BY RUTH ANN MARTINEZ

RUTH ANN MARTINEZ

Ruth Ann Martinez and her husband, Victor, are codirectors of Calvary Ministerial Institute. They oversee the Bible School, teach, supervise construction of new facilities at the school, host a daily radio program and are involved in church planting. She and her husband minister in the United States through conferences and seminars about the family. Ruth is a graduate of Calvary Bible College, and has a ministry to pastors' wives and other women. Her "Women Warriors" seminar ministered to more than 10,000 people in 1996. Ruth is fluent in both Spanish and English.

Mexico is a country that 100 million people call home; and 50 percent of that population is 12 years old or younger. Thirty years ago 75 percent of Mexico's people resided in villages, but today 80 percent live in the cities.

My parents came to Mexico in 1949 from the United States, and served the people for nearly 40 years. They were drawn to Mexico by their burden for the villages, and one of the first places they ministered to was my husband's village.

OPEN DOORS, OPEN HEARTS

When Dad arrived at that 8,000-foot-high village in the mountains, he was amazed to find people living with so few amenities—not even water or lights. He was greeted with the words, "We are a forgotten and neglected people, nobody cares about us up here." But my dad cared, and my heart rejoices that he did.

Those initial words were indelibly marked upon Dad's heart. He would ride 12 hours on horseback, and then travel on foot to the most remote villages. Eventually his time constraints led to aviational evangelizing, dropping gospel tracts over isolated villages. He would buzz over at tree-top level playing contemporary gospel music; and then fly over again dropping tracts—*A Pilot Speaks of God* and *A Pilot Speaks of the End of the World*.

Tract dropping was banned, but the door opened for radio. The airwaves were a powerful tool for reaching the felt needs of the unsaved and creating unity among all Christians. Dad was a pioneer in loving villages into the Kingdom. He longed to see villages, cities and countries living in unity in Christ.

I started doing follow-up for Dad's radio ministry, and was thankful for the overwhelming response we received in the homes we visited. Within a half hour of our arrival, the homes would overflow with people hungry to know more about Jesus.

A TEACHER BORN TO BE HEARD

Growing up in Mexico I saw the broken homes, the alcoholism, the abandoned mothers and hurting children. From the time I was old enough to reason, I knew I had to reach out to them. I had a tremendous burden for the women and children. I started teaching Sunday School when I was 9 years old. By the time I was 13, I was training teachers.

During my teenage years I began to lead a home Bible study for women, which eventually grew to 14 groups a week. They were eager to receive the gospel from me, and I would endeavor to disciple them. But when I attempted to teach the women how to respect their husbands and how to raise their children, I encountered great resistance. They believed I was too young and too inexperienced to understand the reality of their problems. Generally, I found that no one listens to a teenager with no experience.

TODAY THEY LISTEN

Twenty-four years later as a wife and mother—and now grandmother...the women listen.

I married a man with a kindred passion for discipling God's Body. My husband and I invested our efforts at a Bible school, first as teachers, and then as directors. We began with a heart full of gratitude and a fraction of an acre of property. Eventually God generously provided 25 more acres with a mandate to have a "world missions training and sending base." We have plans for a school that will accommodate 1,500 students.

God not only blessed our work at the school, but also multiplied our opportunities to minister. When we were offered a theater in Monterrey, Mexico, we said, "We have nothing to do with buying buildings, or planting churches, our job is to train leaders to reach the world." We were accustomed to our little town, and had nothing to do with the cities.

The owner insisted, saying "We are closing this 1,100-seat theater because it is no longer a prosperous business. Video and satellite have taken over the theater business, and we don't want to replace it with pornography. Please come and see it. You have a large vision." Even greater than our vision was the greatness of our God. We knew that if it was His plan, He would bring it to pass.

Since then we have purchased six theaters, four of which were once pornographic. This in turn opened the door to broadcasting.

When God presented my husband with a radio ministry, I, too, felt the Holy Spirit tugging at my heart to do a radio show for broken, hurting, rejected women.

I especially felt a burden for widows, divorcees, abandoned wives and single mothers. But I wondered if I was equipped for the task. I said, "Lord, I'm not the one because I have a happy marriage and my children love You—I haven't gone through a traumatic situation."

I sensed the Lord saying, *Do you want to wait to become a widow?*

I said, "No, Lord, I'll start now."

OVERCOMING DENOMINATIONAL
BARRIERS THROUGH COMMON NEEDS

My husband and I launched a radio show dealing with contemporary issues that women face. More opportunities began to unfold.
Soon I was hosting breakfasts, luncheons and teas for women. I
became president of Women's Aglow for a year in Monterrey. Our
loving concern for women's needs overcame denominational barriers. Women were uniting around the common factor of need, and
we organized an entire week for women. The idea was to go to
where the women were, whatever their social, economic or religious status.

The theme of our first event in 1991 was "Overcoming Your
Conflicts." Nearly 1,500 ladies were ministered to in 22 meetings during one week.

But that was only the beginning. By 1996 the theme was "Women
Warriors, Let's Take Responsibility for Our Families, Our Nation and
Our World" ministering to 16,000 people. We had 165 meetings with-
in a 350-mile radius during one week with 55 different speakers.

In 1996 Women's Week expanded to Nicaragua and Southern
Mexico. Since March of that year, we have ministered to approximately 6,000 people in that part of our world.

One lady who came to Women's Week eagerly organized the program in her own city three weeks later. She arranged for a meeting
among 280 Indian women in a tin-roofed building. The ladies walked
hours to get to the meeting.

They eventually rented a dance hall, and about 320 ladies came
from every strata of society. Testimonies of what God had done had
spread throughout the area. The day of the meeting, one lady on the
verge of filing for a divorce was driven to her knees shouting, "I will
forgive my husband!" The sound of her knees crashing on the con-
crete floor was so loud, I was convinced she had been hurt. Much to
my astonishment, at that same moment she felt a tumor being
yanked from her womb and felt an intense lingering warmth that
resided in her body for nearly two hours.

An unsaved lady offered to translate when the interpreter failed to
show up. As the speaker spoke the translator became so absorbed in
what she was hearing that she would forget to translate. In the mid-

dle of the message she fell to her knees crying, "I want to give my heart to Jesus."

We have seen time and time again that as the ladies have been healed emotionally, physical healings have followed. Several ladies unable to conceive children returned to the Women's Week the following year proudly carrying their babies, declaring the miraculous intervention of God's love in their lives.

Through Women's Week, many denominational barriers have been broken. I have been invited to city and denominational pastors' meetings all based upon the common factor of women and their needs.

MULTIPLIED BLESSINGS

Our forum for ministry was multiplied in 1996 when God gave us a place we refer to as our prayer mountain—a 230-acre working ranch.

WE CAN CHOOSE TO EITHER LINK SHIELDS, AND IN THAT WAY BECOME AN IMPOSING OFFENSIVE FORCE AGAINST THE ENEMY, OR WE CAN CHOOSE TO WIELD OUR OWN SHIELDS AND SPEND MOST OF OUR TIME ON THE DEFENSIVE.

More than 2,000 people have come to pray, and 500 people have been baptized so far on the prayer mountain. People from all denominations and every nation are welcome to come for prayer and ministry. In addition we have a place for children to come and play, and then pray.

Our greatest burden is for the children. Recognizing that 50 percent of Mexico's population is 12 and under, we also started the first of many bilingual Christian schools in 1996.

Our prayer is that the hearts of the fathers will be turned to the children, and the hearts of the children will be turned to the fathers. We pray that the curse of fatherlessness will be removed from our nation.

One of the six theaters we have purchased since 1989 is located in an area where 96 bars were doing business within a 12-block square. We are happy to report that more than 35 have closed their doors, and the atmosphere in downtown Monterrey has changed.

LINKING SHIELDS

One area of Monterrey has been penetrated by more than 100 churches. As a result the crime rate has diminished, and city officials have had to decrease the police force.

The purchase of the theaters, the miracles of provision, the daily radio broadcasts, the property that serves as a church and family-camp facility, the Christian schools and the many churches that have been blessed as a result of these outreaches provide evidence that God wants His Church networking to increase its effectiveness for the unsaved world.

We have found that we can choose to either link shields, and in that way become an imposing offensive force against the enemy, or we can choose to wield our own shields and spend most of our time on the defensive.

In 1995 we joined as a part of an effort to prayerwalk through the entire city. It was the most concerted act of networking ever attempted in Mexico, and we continue to experience the fruits of that endeavor.

Monterrey is emerging into a world-class city. As a northern city, it sets the pace for the rest of the country. We sense that what God is doing in Monterrey will greatly affect the rest of the country as we link hearts and hands together to meet the common need factor—the need for Jesus.

For more information, contact:
Missionary Revival Crusade
102 East Lyons Street
Laredo, TX 78040
(210) 722-2646

GIVING JESUS TO YOUR NEIGHBORS: *JESUS* VIDEO PROJECT

BY LLOYD OLSON

LLOYD OLSON

Lloyd Olson is executive director of the *JESUS* Video Project, a ministry of Campus Crusade for Christ. He graduated from UCLA and is a certified public accountant. Lloyd's responsibilities with Campus Crusade have included worldwide administrative and financial services to more than 100,000 full-time associates in 154 countries. He has ministered in 40 countries, and consults with the management of several Christian ministries.

WHAT IF...

...you could easily motivate those in your church to share Christ with their neighbors and friends?

...a natural, effective, nonconfrontational gospel presentation could bring 40 percent of those who hear (and see) it come to Christ?

...it ignited joy and enthusiasm in your church?

Would you be interested?

A new neighborhood outreach has brought Christians of diverse backgrounds together to share Christ in communities across the United States. From Birmingham to Syracuse to San Antonio, believers by the thousands are offering the gift of the *JESUS* video to those in every home in their communities.

The *JESUS* film, a dramatization of the Gospel of Luke, is the most widely viewed film in history. Now the 83-minute video version of *JESUS* is leading people to Christ in their own homes—and helping to renew America one neighborhood at a time.

HELP ME, RHONDA

Rhonda Brown and her two children came to faith in Christ through watching the *JESUS* video, and began attending church. Then, her Boulder, Colorado, pastor noticed she was absent from worship for many weeks, and feared she was slipping away from her new found faith. Phone calls and contacts were made to no avail.

One day Rhonda called, and with great excitement explained that her new job initially involved 70 hours a week—a financial blessing she needed as a struggling single mother. She told her pastor she had missed 18 Sunday services. She had been counting!—and also related a fascinating story.

When Rhonda told a struggling neighborhood family how Jesus—through the *JESUS* video—had changed her life, they wanted to see it. One evening she and her boys marched down the street to show the video to their neighbors. The parents and three children all prayed to accept Jesus as their Savior. Now, that family regularly attends church. Rhonda's pastor told some of his congregation, "We've been in church all those 18 weeks. Yet Rhonda, in her absence, has been the most fruitful member of our congregation."

160 EXCITED EVANGELISTS

Pastor John Abbott reports what began in small, rural Colfax, Indiana, and is now spreading across several countries:

"We joined with the other two churches in Colfax and distributed the *JESUS* video to every home (410) that would accept them. We've had 17 people publicly commit their lives to Jesus in baptism at our services since the video went out. I have 160 evangelists in my church now who are excited about sharing the gospel because for once they have the answer in their hands as they talk.

"We have turned our rural town to Christ and they continue to come. We used to have 20 or 25 show up for prayer meetings. We now have about 100 showing up, and the prayers aren't about Aunt Sue's broken toe. They're praying for souls—with tears."

A HARVEST OF SOULS

The Syracuse *JESUS* video project is a large-scale, multi-church effort that distributed 28,750 videos. Five months later, independent market research found that 96 percent of those who viewed the video appreciated the effort and said to the churches, "keep it up!" Of course Syracuse, New York is not in the Bible Belt. Yet the surprising findings revealed that:

- Sixty-seven percent of those who received a video watched it.
- Forty-three percent of those who watched it prayed the prayer at the end.
- Seventy-five percent of those who prayed the prayer reported positive changes in their lives as a result of their decision.
- Twenty-six percent of those praying the prayer started attending a church.
- And, in each household 3.65 people watched the video.

People want JESUS! Nationwide, more than 2,600 churches and 87,000 workers in 82 cities have approached 1.7 million homes and have given more than 700,000 videos as free gifts. More than 700,000 people have made decisions for Christ. Churches of all stripes have been involved—Baptist, Lutheran, Methodist, Presbyterian, Nazarene and more. Already, three denominations (Southern Baptist, Assemblies of God and Evangelical Free) have adopted the *JESUS* video project as a national emphasis.

Giving a video to someone is natural and nonthreatening. A major American evangelist recently noted, "In this generation, the stadium is not the number one vehicle for leading people to Christ. People like to stay at home nights and be comfortable." Television screens in the average American home are lit up more than seven hours each day. The *JESUS* video is tactful and fruitful. It uses God's Word, which He said "shall not return to Me empty" (Isa. 55:11).

Scripture tells us to "love your neighbor as yourself" (Luke 10:27). Can we really love our neighbors without offering Jesus to them? How will you reach your neighborhood?...Your Jerusalem?...Your city or state? How will the Great Commission be fulfilled by the year 2000? *It will only happen if we Christians go to the lost.*

Reaching your city requires churches working together. Churches may take *JESUS* videos to a zip code, a neighborhood, a thousand homes surrounding their church, an apartment complex in a decaying neighborhood or subsidized housing complexes. Members can give them to visitors, coworkers, social acquaintances, merchants and government officials. This list of possibilities is as long as the number of non-Christians in your world. The goal is to get the Word of God on video into every home possible. This is the video generation.

JUST TRY IT

May I encourage you to try this creative outreach? Order 50 or 100 videos; give them away, and see what happens. Maybe God will prompt you to lead an outreach in your neighborhood, church or city. A tremendous need still exists for committed leaders to make it happen in their cities.

Billy Graham told a group of evangelists, "I think historians will look back—and say that this time has been a period of revival. Wouldn't it be something if you slept through the revival?" Don't sleep through it! The harvest is now!

For more information about the *JESUS* video:
See the JVP home page on the Internet:
http://www.mdalink.com/JESUSvideo
E-mail: jesusvideo@aol.com
Fax: 909-881-7779
Phone: 800-29JESUS
Write: JESUS Video Project, 24600
         Arrowhead Springs Road, San Bernardino, CA 92414

PUTTING FEET TO OUR WORDS: MARCH FOR JESUS USA

BY TOM PELTON

TOM PELTON

Tom Pelton is the founder, president and national coordinator for March for Jesus USA. He has traveled nationally and internationally, speaking at churches and conferences with the message of unity and the significance of worship. He has trained hundreds of leaders to unite and mobilize their cities. He has been a regular guest on CBN and TBN. Tom has been in full time ministry for 17 years as a youth pastor, worship leader and pastor. Throughout his ministry, he planned many events for those who would not normally go to a church building.

March for Jesus is a national and international event that unites the entire Body of Christ in cities throughout the world for one purpose: to worship Jesus. The March calls Christians of all denominations to take the joy of knowing Jesus beyond the Church walls and into the streets with praise and prayer.

March for Jesus is not a protest, not politically motivated and has no hidden agenda. We come together joyfully to celebrate the Lord

Jesus Christ and to pray for our cities and nations. March for Jesus is entirely for Jesus.

UNITY AROUND OUR HIGHEST
COMMON DENOMINATOR

Churches rise above differences to come together in the One we all have in common—the Lord Jesus Christ. March for Jesus helps build strong relationships and unity among churches.

The Church outside its walls worshiping Jesus in public makes the event a demonstration of our love for God, our love for one another and our love for the cities where we live. Taking the walls off the Church makes us visible, accessible and reminds everyone of God's great love for all people.

A WORLD TO WIN TOGETHER

March for Jesus symbolizes the whole Church taking the whole gospel to the whole world. The Global March is a catalyst for the kind of extraordinary prayer, unity through cooperation and mobilization that will be required to reach the world with the good news of Jesus Christ.

WHAT HAPPENS AT A MARCH FOR JESUS?

The primary expression at a March for Jesus is celebration. It is much like a family gathering. Children especially enjoy the March. Local authorities report that March for Jesus is a pleasant and well organized event that is always welcome in their communities.

Christians gather to march down their city streets. The March music, arranged for the outdoor expression of our faith, contains songs, prayers and proclamations. With the songbook and prayerscript, every marcher sings to the music broadcast through mobile sound systems. The March concludes with a Prayer Rally led by local pastors.

WHO ORGANIZES A MARCH FOR JESUS?

March for Jesus USA does not appoint the March Organizer in a city. A March Organizer is a person appointed or approved by a local group of pastors, called the Pastors Steering Committee. The March Organizer is under the authority and spiritual protection of the Pastors Steering Committee. The March Organizer works closely with a March Organizational Committee, which handles the management of the details of the March. The Committee oversees the various task groups. Task Group Leaders are needed to organize these teams of people who concentrate on specific tasks.

MARCHES IN ENGLAND

The Marches in England began in the 1980s when some small churches decided to take what they were experiencing in their churches out into the streets. Songwriter Graham Kendrick participated in some of these early attempts, and wrote a series of songs appropriate for the outdoor expression of the Church.

MARCHES IN THE UNITED STATES

In 1989, my wife and I attended a worship leaders conference in California where Graham Kendrick presented the March vision. I shared the vision with a group of pastors in my home city, and after two praise marches, we set up March for Jesus USA to help coordinate and organize USA Marches. Many cities in the United States began preparing for the first national March for Jesus on May 23, 1992.

During the first Global March for Jesus on June 25, 1994, 1.5 million believers marched on the streets of 550 cities in America's third March for Jesus. That day, a total of 10 million people marched down the streets of 1,500 cities in 178 nations throughout the world to the glory and praise of God. Millions of believers from every time zone in the world proclaimed that "From the rising of the sun to the place where it sets, the name of the Lord is to be praised" (Ps. 113:3).

MAY 25, 1996: A WORLD TO WIN TOGETHER

The 1996 Global March for Jesus held on May 25 drew together 10 to 12 million Christians around the world to celebrate Jesus on the streets of more than 2,000 cities in 170 nations. An estimated 1 million marched in 625 cities throughout the United States.

Some of the larger Marches across the nation were: 40,000 in Nashville, Tennessee; 21,000 in Toledo, Ohio; 20,000 in Miami, Florida; 18,000 in Jacksonville, Florida; and 18,000 in Pittsburgh, Pennsylvania.

The governors of California, Georgia, Louisiana, Nevada, New York and West Virginia all proclaimed May 25 as March for Jesus Day. Dozens of mayors did the same in their cities.

THE FUTURE OF MARCH FOR JESUS

In the year 2000, parties and celebrations will occur across the planet. Whether people know it or not, they will be celebrating the 2000th birthday of Jesus Christ. Let's make it possible for the whole world to know, with a glorious and extravagant Global March for Jesus in that year.

Also in the year 2000, we want to be celebrating great advances made in the final years of this millennium toward the completion of the Great Commission. Each March for Jesus will be a celebration of God's kingdom advancing.

The procession itself is a powerful prophetic symbol of our progress together for the gospel. Being on the streets symbolizes taking the walls off the Church to make the gospel message more available to the people. Such united prayer and praise can change the world. What better way for the Body of Christ to celebrate His 2000 years!

To help mobilize your city for Jesus, write or call:
March for Jesus USA
Box 3216
Austin, TX 78764
Phone: (512) 416-0066

RELATIONSHIPS TO OTHER CHRISTIAN DENOMINATIONS: DIVERSE BODY, ONE MESSAGE

BY DON ARGUE

DON ARGUE

Don Argue, Ed.D., is president of the National Association of Evangelicals (NAE), which is comprised of about 42,500 congregations nationwide. He has served as president of North Central College, Minneapolis, Minnesota since 1979. As a result of Dr. Argue's leadership, the college received the Christianity Today Decade of Growth Award for being the fastest growing college of its kind in the 1980s. In prior years he served as dean of students and campus pastor at Evangel College. He was also pastor of churches in San Jose and Morgan Hill, California.

This is a *kairos* moment for the Church of Jesus Christ. At the close of the twenty-first century, the Church exists in a world tortured by polarization, selfishness, indifference and godlessness. Furthermore, the Church, particularly the Body of Christ in America, despite its significant influence and ministry, has been so infected by such sins that it has a witness and ministry for Christ far less than it could or should be. In this day, however, the critical need for greater unity and godliness among Christians is being met with a surging desire for just such a transformation. And, it is springing up across the breadth of the Church.

It could well be that the Body of Christ is ready now to allow the pastoral prayer of the Son of God in John 17:20-23 to renew itself dramatically in our lives:

> *"My prayer is not for them alone. I pray also for those who will believe in me through their message, that all of them may be one, Father, just as you are in me and I am in you. May they also be in us so that the world may believe that you have sent me. I have given them the glory that you gave me, that they may be one as we are one: I in them and you in me. May they be brought to complete unity to let the world know that you sent me and have loved them even as you have loved me."*

This could result in a sharpened witness for Christ, and a strengthened service to those in need.

The Church of Christ is receiving a wake-up call to work together across denominational lines in a spirit of unity. The desired results to this call to action are to glorify God, to strengthen our witness to those who do not know Jesus Christ as Lord and Savior, and to expand and improve our ministry to the world.

TODAY'S CALL FOR ACTION:
CALL FOR PRAYER—PRELUDE TO
EFFECTIVE MINISTRY

> *"Have faith in God," Jesus answered. "I tell you the truth, if anyone says to this mountain, 'Go, throw yourself into the sea,' and does not doubt in his heart but believes that what he says will happen, it will be done for him. Therefore I tell you, whatever you ask for in prayer, believe that you have received it, and it will be yours. And when you stand praying, if you hold anything against anyone, forgive him, so that your Father in heaven may forgive your sins" (Mark 11:22-25).*

Christians are called to pray for unity and for the spread of the gospel. Prayer involves worshiping and praising God; calling upon Him; confessing our sin and need for His grace; seeking His wisdom and counsel; interceding for others; and offering ourselves to Him for His service.

Pastors are encouraged to become involved in local, regional and national prayer endeavors. Reaching cities with the gospel will require cooperative efforts among its churches. And prayer is the prelude to effective ministry.

Today the Holy Spirit is bringing together prayer networks and prayer ministries throughout the United States. Pastors in many local communities are meeting for prayer one day a month, and the results have been felt in their communities.

CALL FOR REPENTANCE AND REFORM

"If my people who are called by my name will humble themselves, and pray and seek my face, and turn from their wicked ways, then will I hear from heaven, and will forgive their sin and will heal their land" (2 Chron. 7:14, NKJV).

As Christians we should humbly and publicly follow the guidelines of 2 Chronicles 7:14 and confess...

- Although we have been conscientious in our response to the mandate of the Great Commission to go and make disciples (see Matt. 28:18-20; Mark 16:15), we have too often failed to live out and actualize the mandate of a loving unity, which testifies to our Lord Jesus (see John 13:34,35; John 17:21,22).
- Although we value unity and united Christian action, we too often do more to build our own ministries than to cooperate in making it difficult for people in our own neighborhoods to be lost for eternity.
- That in our pursuit of faithfulness, we have too often accommodated the spirit of this world, which elevates a political correctness over the more difficult task of critical reflection and repentance.
- That although we have assented to Christian truths as

embodied in our Assemblies of God statement of faith, we have on many occasions been unwilling to be confronted redemptively with the implications of biblical truths about life and faith.

- That although we exist to serve the ministry at the local church, we have not done all we can to advance wholly biblical understanding of the Church and the Lord's mandates—in evangelism, or in reconciliation.

The Church is called to repentance in the pursuit of revival and renewal through prayer and fasting, and through faithfulness to God in every aspect of our lives as commanded in Scripture.

The Church is called to pursue the fruit of the Spirit manifested in reconciliation—to God and to each other.

CALL FOR UNITY AND COOPERATION—THE COMMAND ACTUALIZED

"A new command I give you: Love one another. As I have loved you, so you must love one another. By this all men will know that you are my disciples, if you love one another" (John 13:34,35).

Bible believing churches in a community are called to work together diligently as a reflection of their common commitment to Jesus Christ as Lord and Savior. Furthermore, as long as the truth is not compromised, believers are urged, in a demonstration of love, to work alongside others who may not necessarily have a Pentecostal identity on various specific issues.

Pastors should lead in facilitating and supporting united evangelical endeavors. They must, however, maintain the authority of the Bible. Evangelism is effective in demonstrating unity only when it is based on biblical truths.

A. Local and Regional Action

"But you will receive power when the Holy Spirit comes on you; and you will be my witnesses in Jerusalem, and in all Judea and Samaria" (Acts 1:8).

The ministry of the Church is essentially local. Therefore pastors are encouraged at the local and regional levels to provide and carry out strategic cooperation in prayer, evangelism and discipleship to reach the lost in a particular area. Leaders in the local church are encouraged to demonstrate godly, reconciling love as together they proclaim God's Word.

Pastors are encouraged to use a leadership strategy, which includes the following five principles from Ted Haggard's book *Primary Purpose* (Creation House), in an approach of cooperation without compromise:

- Focus on the absolutes of the Christian faith.
- Promote the ministry of Christ and His Word above your own ministry or method.
- Pray to raise the level of the Holy Spirit's activity in your area.
- Appreciate one another's gifts in ministry.
- Practice supportive speech and actions toward one another.

B. National Action

"And to the ends of the earth" (Acts 1:8).

Pastors are called to lead their churches to operate in cooperation without compromise—maintaining their particular distinctives, yet standing together on the basis of the Lord Jesus Christ's command found in John 13:34,35.

CALL FOR EVANGELISM—THE MANDATE REALIZED

"All authority in heaven and on earth has been given to me. Therefore go and make disciples of all nations, baptizing them in the name of the Father and of the Son and of the Holy Spirit, and teaching them to obey everything I have commanded you. And surely I am with you always, to the very end of the age" (Matt 28:18-20).

The pastor and local church are called to work together with others, according to Christ's paradigm. They are to demonstrate reconciling love through an integrated agenda of cooperative evangelism and discipleship.

The implications of this call require more than the agenda of one local church. They require evangelicals to unify across biblically value-based, broad horizons of cooperation to reach the lost.

CALL FOR CULTURAL IMPACT

"You are the salt of the Earth, but if the salt loses its saltiness, how can it be made salty again? It is no longer good for anything, except to be thrown out and trampled by men. You are the light of the world. A city on a hill cannot be hidden. Neither do people light a lamp and put it under a bowl. Instead they put it on its stand, and it gives light to everyone in the house. In the same way, let your light shine before men, that they may see your good deeds and praise your Father in heaven" (Matt. 5:13-16).

The Church is called to be faithful, and to rely wholly upon the power of God to transform our lives, our churches and our communities. We can make no greater impact on the world than simply being the faithful, vibrant, worshiping, evangelizing and loving community Christ has redeemed.

Christians are encouraged to engage fully their duel citizenship (heaven and earth), exercising their rights and privileges freely to pray and participate in the national democratic form of government.

As churches work together in unity across denominational lines, they must seek to nurture, encourage and facilitate fidelity to the Word of God—incarnate, revealed and proclaimed!

"Now to him who is able to do immeasurably more than all we ask or imagine, according to his power that is at work within us, to him be glory in the church and in Christ Jesus throughout all generations, for ever and ever! Amen (Eph. 3:20,21).

You may contact NAE in the following ways:
Mail: NAE, P.O. Box 28, Wheaton, IL 60189
Phone: (630) 665-0500   E-Mail nae@nae.net
Fax   (630) 665-8575   www: http://www.nae.net

IMPACT PRODUCTIONS

BY TOM NEWMAN

TOM NEWMAN

Tom Newman is president of Impact Productions, a production company focused on communicating God's love through the performing arts, television and film. He has an international reputation of uncompromised message and artistic excellence. As a producer, Tom has presented numerous works for the stage and television in the United States and abroad. As a stage and screen actor, he often plays the role of Jesus. He is a featured speaker at mission conferences and youth events. Tom resides in Tulsa with his wife, Susan, and four children.

The most recognized image or individual in today's world is not Jesus Christ, or a world leader—it's none other than Ronald McDonald. Our first impulse when hearing this may be to protest and complain that a fictitious fast-food character occupies the place where Jesus should be. In television, music, major films, concerts and the performing arts, the distortions are much the same. We protest and complain about the impropriety of the world's messages and messengers filling our televisions, movie screens, stages and concert halls with their values and lifestyles because they don't reflect ours.

COMMUNICATING IN TERMS THEY WILL UNDERSTAND

But all of our justifiable protesting has set us back years in technology and production; and the world looks at us as a protesting movement.

CHRISTIANS HAVE NOT BEEN PLACED HERE TO CURSE THE DARKNESS, BUT TO BE SALT AND LIGHT.

Christians have not been placed here to curse the darkness, but to be salt and light. We cannot expect the world to reflect our values unless we have first reached them with the love and message of Christ.

We must speak to our world in terms they will understand. "If I don't speak your language, then I cannot communicate with you. If I cannot communicate with you, then you will be unable to receive what I have to say—thus the relational gap between secular and spiritual America" (Randall Parr, *Ministries Today*, June 1994).

Now more than ever we must be diligent to impact our culture. Our society is not only being devoured through governments and legal systems, but also through diabolic drugs and the ungodly influences of the world. When we see that more than 100 billion dollars a year are spent on illegal drugs in this country alone, we recognize the minimal impact laws actually have.

RAISING UP A STANDARD

The hearts and souls of the world we live in are being won by those who control our culture. I'm not simply referring to the entertainment business, but I am also talking about what and who will determine not only what clothes we will wear, what style of haircuts we will copy, what cars we will drive, but also and even more importantly what lifestyles and morals we will embrace.

The battlefield reaches beyond the entertainment business. It extends to the fight for the hearts and souls of the human race. The messages ingested today through movies, dramas, television and music will dictate what the world will become tomorrow. The Bible assures us that "when [Satan] shall come in like a flood, the Spirit of the Lord shall lift up a standard against him" (Isa. 59:19, *KJV*). We have all recognized the flood of evil. Now is the time for the righteous standard to be raised. Impact Productions is committed to fight in this arena. This generation belongs to God, and we intend to claim it for His inheritance.

Wherever Jesus went, He caused a commotion. Wherever our performances, films, commercials, training or music are presented, we believe they too will cause a commotion. Not so much with what people will observe, but more importantly in the spiritual realm where we believe Satan and the kingdom of darkness are put to flight as we lift up Jesus and His truth.

We realize that our warfare in not against flesh and blood, but against principalities and powers in high places. Using the tools of film, dance, drama and technology, we can speak the language of the world. By combining these with the creativity placed in us by God, we can incorporate the most powerful message of all.

IN OUR BEGINNING...

Impact Productions began 15 years ago with a drama entitled *Toymaker and Son*. Through its development into *The Masterpiece* over the years, we have had the opportunity of performing in 27 nations, ministering to more than 3 million in live-performance settings, resulting in nearly 300,000 public declarations to Christ. *The Masterpiece* continues to be performed 160 times each year.

Impact Productions has joined with Wycliffe Bible translators and the International Festival of the Arts to begin touring with *Dayuma*, a dramatic dance production of the Jim Elliott story, as told in *Through the Gates of Splendor*. We are praying this production will be the catalyst for launching a brand new wave of missionaries and Bible translators into the field for the end-time harvest.

WORDS ARE NOT ENOUGH

The best-loved cult in America is the Mormon church. How have they accomplished this task? Through their brilliant development of television commercials. They say in warm fuzzy images that family and God are significant to our lives.

We have developed more than 25 hard-hitting, Christ-elevating commercials. We have made these available for churches to use throughout the country. Every day more than 20 million Americans are being confronted with the life-giving message and directed to life-giving churches. The response from television stations, churches, combined with church growth has been staggering.

Sermons delivered through words only, often fall short in reaching those entertained by the movies, videos, television and high-tech performances the world continually offers. Dramatic Impact is the missions and drama training division of Impact Productions. It trains the Oral Roberts University summer missions students and develops dramas for Teen Mania ministries, Big World Ventures and many churches to minister powerfully in foreign countries where language would be a hindrance to effective ministry.

Impact also works with pastors in developing illustrated sermons. As the pastor speaks, we visually enhance the message with sketches, props and video projection, bringing the story to life.

We have produced entertaining and informative television specials that focus on the questions people ask. From *Death and Beyond*, to our most recent piece *Hymns*, we help answer the questions of a world paralyzed by fear about death, bringing them comfort through the most beloved hymns. These are hymns that are sung by more than 200 million people each week around the world. Multiplied thousands have come to Christ as these works have been aired worldwide in nine different languages. We are currently producing short films from Max Lucado's and Ron DiCianni's *Tell Me the Stories*.

A SYNERGISTIC BLAST THAT IMPACTS THE WORLD

Impact Productions was birthed out of a necessity to reveal God's truth to a generation shaped by the sight-and-sound influences of its culture. Impact is an assembling of multi-talented and called individuals whose commitment is to God, and whose expression of their commitment is their art.

Impact is defined by its name, with the spirit, talent and focus of individuals working as a synergistic blast that impacts the world we live in with the message that God is not only alive, but He is also relevant and able to meet every need. We want to fight on the cultural battlefield. For too long, we have stayed out of the fight. We believe we can effectively wage war in this arena and win.

For more information contact:

Impact Productions
3939 South Harvard
Tulsa, OK 74135   E-mail: impactprod@aol.com
Phone: (918) 746-0888   Internet: http://www.impactprod.org
Toll free: (800) 422-7863 Fax: (918) 746-0847

TOM NEWMAN

LIGHTS OVER HOUSTON

BY ALICE SMITH

ALICE SMITH

Alice Smith is the prayer coordinator of The U.S. Prayer Track of the A.D. 2000 and Beyond Movement, and Mission America. She is editor of the "Watchmen National Prayer Alert" newsletter and "PrayerNet," a weekly internet publication. Alice and her husband, Eddie, coordinator of the U.S. Prayer Track, make their home in Houston, Texas. They travel internationally teaching in conferences and seminars.

BREAKTHROUGH HOUSTON

October 30, 1990, is a night to remember. A historic moment occurred as Houston-area pastors and churches gathered in the coliseum to pray for revival and spiritual awakening. The event, called "Breakthrough Houston," was the idea of Dr. Reginald Klimionok, pastor of Evangelistic Temple in Houston, Texas. However, it involved dozens of churches representing various denominations and ethic groups.

For several months committees met, pastors prayed and plans were laid for the special event. The cooperating churches and parachurch ministries participated in a three-day "PowerFast" leading up to Tuesday night. At dusk, thousands of Houstonians emerged from the underground parking areas, and filed their way into the coliseum.

Christians from many denominations and worship styles burst into the huge auditorium filled with joyous praise! Pastors, charismatic and noncharismatic, evangelical and liturgical, met first backstage for prayer; and then made their way to seats on the giant stage. The atmosphere was "electric."

THE POWER OF CORPORATE PRAYER

The program consisted of a blending of praise and worship and intercession. Between times of worship, pastors were assigned to speak briefly and pray for various subjects. Corporately the city's Church in Houston repented for its sin.

We repented for our personal sins, and for the sins of our fellow citizens as well. We prayed prayers of replacement, asking God to replace the spirit of pride with a spirit of humility; the spirit of racism with a spirit of acceptance; the spirit of anger and violence with a spirit of peace.

We prayed petitionary prayers for pastors and churches, children and homes, schools and universities, businesses and industry. We earnestly cried out for God to break the cycle of crime in our city. As each worship set finished and each prayer was completed, the corporate spirit grew with intensity.

Each person was given a prayer covenant and a corporate declaration we were to announce to principalities above the city. Around 8:45 P.M., we read the covenant of unity and prayer in unison. Then authoritatively, we read the declaration to break the power of the enemy over Houston. The coliseum seemed to tremble as the shout of thousands of Christians roared heavenward! We all had a sense that somehow spiritual strongholds had been broken. However, having only a subjective opinion of our supposed breakthrough, objective facts were needed to prove our discerned opinion. So we asked the Lord for confirmation. We concluded the evening by taking communion together.

EVIDENCE OF BREAKTHROUGH

Two days later, on November 1, a news report entitled "What Were Those Lights in the Sky?" appeared in the *Houston Chronicle* on page 28A. The article read as follows:

> According to some accounts, it definitely was a burning aircraft that crashed and exploded in the Tomball (Northwest Houston) area....It was the stuff of an unsolved Halloween mystery, but authorities agreed that the UFO sighted in northwest Harris County and southwest Montgomery County on Tuesday night probably resulted from a meteor shower. Still, area law enforcement agencies, as well as fire stations, had no choice but to take the reports that came in about 8:45 P.M. seriously.

To those of us who had participated in Breakthrough Houston, this was a confirming sign in the heavenlies. However, further confirmation was to be noted.

From that night, crime in the city of Houston began to decrease. In December 1994, the *Houston Post* reported that violent crime had dropped 29.2 percent since January 1991. By 1995, the *Houston Chronicle* reported crime had dropped an additional 31.9 percent to a record decrease of 51.1 percent! This level has been maintained during the first six months of 1996!

AMERICA, A NATION IN NEED OF LIGHT

Today, my husband Eddie Smith, coordinator of The U.S. PRAYER TRACK, and I turn our attention to a larger concern, the worsening spiritual condition of the United States, our "Jerusalem." Our nation's moral torch is burning low. America stands in desperate need of revival.

We are giving ourselves to coordinate PrayUSA!—a cooperative effort to "bring the United States to its knees" for 30 days in prayerful repentance and fasting for revival and spiritual awakening each April. A strategic alliance of thousands of individual, neighborhood and local church prayer ministries and hundreds of national prayer mobilizers, PrayUSA! is a national prayer initiative of Mission America.

Our PrayUSA! Committee, chaired by Steve Bell, executive director of Concerts of Prayer International, comprises scores of national and regional prayer leaders.

Enlisted as strategic partners will be denominational and non-denominational, church and parachurch prayer ministries. They will agree to plan specific, measurable prayer initiatives to mobilize prayer specifically for revival and spiritual awakening in the United States each April. These partners will serve the intercessors of the United States by providing prayer resources specific to their ministries. They will promote PrayUSA! among their constituencies via their newsletters, publications and media broadcasts.

Besides the participation in the United States, the A.D. 2000 United PRAYER TRACK, under the leadership of C. Peter Wagner, will seek to mobilize prayer and fasting for the United States globally.

Our goal is that through strategic partnerships, we can mobilize worldwide, massive, focused, fervent prayer for the United States. We believe this will result in true revival in the Church, evidenced by national spiritual awakening with a tremendous harvest of souls! Today we are praying for lights over America!

For information, or to order a Press Kit ($10), contact:

Eddie Smith, Coordinator
PrayUSA!
7710-T Cherry Park Drive, Suite 224
Houston, TX 77095

8

GROW TOGETHER

TIDES UP, BOATS RISE TOGETHER
BY TED HAGGARD

Have you noticed that fast food restaurants are often grouped together? When McDonald's builds a restaurant on one corner, if the population, product and service remain consistent, a certain market level will be established in the community. One method for increasing sales is grouping restraurants together. When Burger King builds a restaurant on an adjacent corner, McDonald's income may temporarily decline as people discover the new Burger King; but eventually, both McDonald's and Burger King will reap increased business.

If all things remain equal, in order for McDonald's and Burger King to increase their profits, Wendy's must build on the third corner. McDonald's and Burger King may experience a temporary dip in sales, but ultimately, both McDonald's and Burger King will have more sales. The three restaurants grouped together will attract more business than if they were separated from one another.

Businesses cluster their offices in increasingly taller buildings in downtown areas, and retailers thrive in malls with competing stores to spawn greater success. Financial markets are grouped together on Wall Street, moviemakers in Hollywood and automobile manufacturers in Detroit. Although major exceptions to this principle do exist, the primary concept remains true: *Groupings of successful businesses create a synergy of success.*

That same principle is true for our local churches. In some communities, thriving churches with expanding effectiveness are common and expected. In others, however, future projections for strong church growth are dismal. People know that if the water is going up, all the boats rise. But if it's going down, they all go down. The goal of praying together, planning together and implementing His plan is to cause the water level in your city to rise, and thus, cause all of the life-giving churches in your community to rise with it.

RAISE THE WATER LEVEL

As we discovered in chapter 4, the water level of the Holy Spirit's activity in our cities is the percentage of our city's population attending a life-giving church on an average Sunday morning.[1] In Colorado Springs, our goal is to:

1. Pray for every person in our city at least once a year;
2. Communicate the gospel, in an understandable way, to every person within our population at least once a year; and
3. Raise the water level of the Holy Spirit's activity at least 1 percent each year for the next 10 years.

Note that this third goal is reaching 1 percent of the city's population with the gospel, and assimilating them into life-giving churches. Because the city's population is so much larger than the total church population, raising the water level in our city 1 percent may translate into a 5 to 50 percent church-growth rate per year.

Achieving these goals in Colorado Springs requires our network of churches to pray, evangelize and devote itself to communitywide, conversion-based church growth. This raises the water level in our city, causing all of our boats to rise together.

Our city has a population of 350,000 people with approximately 164 life-giving churches. To raise the water level 1 percent, we have to lead at least 3,500 additional people to Christ each year, and assimilate them into our regular church life. That would require the average church to reach at least 21 new people each year, or about 2 per month. The larger ones would reach more, and the smaller ones would probably reach fewer.

But these goals are good for all of us—they keep us focused and on track. Last Sunday night we baptized 90 people; three months prior we baptized 198. Because of intentional citywide goals, I have a greater reason than individual church growth to assimilate these new believers: I need the water level in our entire city to increase. We need to have 164 churches growing in our city for all to be successful. That motivates me.

This mind-set abolishes the negative comparisons among churches. Because we as a corporate Body must reach and disciple 3,500 new people yearly, we all become grateful for each success within the Body of Christ in the city. Every evangelistic effort, every successful television commercial or radio presentation promoting Christ and His Word is a positive contribution to the whole. We realize that for all of our churches to grow, we must constantly pray for the people in our city; plan and implement our strategies; and utilize every opportunity to get the gospel into our community at large.

No longer does presenting the gospel message through a *JESUS* video or a 30-second Impact Productions television spot seem like a bother. It is now a necessity! No longer are we lacking the time to strategize with the other Christian leaders. It is now a necessity! If the water level is rising, everyone involved rises together.

IS THERE A LIMIT TO OUR POTENTIAL GROWTH?

I remember when analysts said the stock market could never exceed 2,000 points. When it approached 3,000, a plethora of books were published portending a collapse of the global marketplace. As 4,000 and 5,000 were exceeded, it became apparent that the opening mar-

kets from the demise of communism and technological breakthroughs were creating virtually unlimited growth.

But now, with the market topping 6,000 points, some still maintain
that the value of multi-national corporations cannot be strong
enough to endure, much less proliferate. I maintain that as long as
people need goods and services, those companies who service them
will increase in value. When populations expand and new products
are in demand, growth is ahead.

As a youth pastor, I hung a chart on my wall listing the local high
schools and the number of students attending those schools.
Whenever someone would comment on the success of our youth
group, I would counter with the number of students not attending
any youth group. My motive was to remind them that a huge number of young people were still unreached in our community. Even
though we had a large group, the growth potential was virtually
unlimited. The need in our community was so great that if we'd had
10 groups our size, we would still have experienced room for growth.
Our youth group was called TAG. I referred to the unreached students of our city as TAG Targets. They were our potential.

This "unlimited potential" concept perpetuated growth among
the youth ministries in our city during those years. We maintained
that the Lord wanted to reach many more students with the gospel,
and that we could all grow simultaneously. There was no shortage.
So to compare ourselves among ourselves became foolish. We
stopped doing it, and instead, realized that we all needed to reach the
junior high and high school students with greater efficacy.

This attitude immunized us from developing problems that often
keep churches from growing. When churches believe the potential
for growth is limited, fear usually takes root. The erroneous belief is
that if any one ministry gets a large portion of the pie, there will be
less for everyone else. In this environment, negative competition is
inevitable and, even though words might be gracious, the reality is
that a jealousy for recognition, influence and growth is cultivated.

Never would any thinking Christian publicly embrace or endorse
these sinful perspectives about ministry. But this atmosphere does pre-
vail in many leaders' hearts. Too often a subtle satisfaction and smug-
ness develop when believers are transferring from another church to
their own. Self-righteousness and high-mindedness often develop.

And, oh do these leaders suffer internally when they are forced to appear pleased about the success of another minister or ministry, especially if they are close friends or associates. They wear happy masks, but in reality are eating their hearts out. They don't want others to be successful because they believe that another person's success is somehow an indicator of their own failure. They secretly enjoy another ministry's failure.

Abundance mentality is the opposite. It springs from the assurance of our roles in God's kingdom. As we observe the potential abundant harvest and its unlimited possibilities, we can gain the emotional and spiritual strength for mutual growth and development. Praying, communicating and working together can all be directed toward growth in all of our churches. With the strength of

A CHOICE FOR UNHEALTHY COMPETITION INFECTS THE BODY AND MAY PRODUCE DEATH. INSTEAD WE SHOULD CHOOSE TO EVALUATE WHETHER OR NOT WE ARE BEING AS EFFECTIVE AS HE WANTS US TO BE SO WE CAN BRING GREATER LIFE TO HIS BODY.

integrity, maturity and a revelation of plentiful harvest fields, positive interaction overcomes right or wrong technique. Work, even poorly conceived and executed, can be successful in a faith-charged atmosphere that is pleasing to the Holy Spirit.

CAN ALL THESE BOATS RISE TOGETHER?

When the tide rises in your community, most of the boats will rise. However, some won't. Successful malls include scores of shops making substantial profits, but as that happens some stores do go out of business. Occasionally a McDonald's or Wendy's provides poor service and loses a major share of its business to its competitors. When that happens, either changes must be made or the business will fail.

The same is true with churches in a community.

People doing comparative shopping among local churches is as much a fact of life as competition between Sears and J.C. Penney or AT&T and MCI. Ultimately, when people get up on Sunday mornings, they choose to go to one church or another. In addition, they choose the church that will be the recipient of their tithes; the one they will volunteer to assist; the church they will pray for; brag about publicly; and the one they will refer friends to. One church will be chosen instead of another.

We choose our responses to this dilemma, and that decision will help us see our own motives: Are we building God's kingdom or having to protect our own? What are we doing? We have all seen the pain and adverse effects produced by competitive attitudes within an individual local church, or among the churches in a city. A choice for unhealthy competition infects the Body and may produce death. Instead we should choose to evaluate whether or not we are being as effective as He wants us to be so we can bring greater life to His Body.

A godly response to comparisons can provide great benefit to our ministries. Hebrews 10:24,25 touches on some of the benefits of positive group dynamics within the Body by saying, "And let us consider how we may spur one another on towards love and good deeds. Let us not give up meeting together, as some are in the habit of doing, but let us encourage one another—and all the more as you see the Day approaching."

Obviously, the Bible is exhorting all of us to intentionally meet together and encourage one another. But I believe we can extrapolate from this verse, the responsibility we all have to force both positive and negative aspects of ministry to spur us on toward love and good deeds. Comparisons others make about our churches could discourage all of us. But through a series of good choices we can change a potentially negative and deadly dynamic into a positive source of hope and life. We must. Why? Because the Day is indeed approaching.

Three of the positive insights we can gain from the comparisons of others include:

1. *An opportunity to measure our effectiveness at communicating the gospel to the unreached.*

If the Lord is bringing visitors to our church and they are responding to the gospel, then we know that we are effective in communicating an eternal truth within a changing culture. If we are reaching people and they are growing into the life of our church, then our prayers and presentations are working.

But sometimes we don't see many visitors in our services and, when we do, the visitors don't respond to our presentation of the gospel. Many rationales can be provided for this, but because the Lord loves the lost so much, if we persist in poor communication with the unreached, He will raise up another body of believers that will successfully communicate to them.

When this happens, we should be challenged to improve the way we communicate. That might mean we need to learn from those who are doing a better job, or at least reconsider our past approach. But it is imperative that we communicate effectively to our society.

As I write this, I can hear the uproar of protest defending our lack of conversion growth and our previous methods. But, even though our defenses may be reasonable, they may ultimately be proven wanting as a neighboring church is used by God to reach the lost. I don't believe God is in a hurry about much except winning the lost. We need to be constantly changing and improving our methods for reaching the unsaved and integrating these new converts into our church body.

2. An opportunity to assess whether or not we are feeding people good food from the Bible.

People come to worship services for various reasons. Most people, though, will only come consistently if they are being spiritually fed.

Again, God might use others' judgments to help us see that often the people who attend our churches are not interested in the same subjects as we pastors. Because their time is valuable and their lives are pressed, people require that we offer something useful to them: principles from God's Word that are applicable to their own lives and a spiritual dynamic that brings life to these principles. If we refuse to teach eternal truth from God's Word or allow for godly worship, then those who are spiritually hungry will go where they can be fed.

3. An opportunity to identify potential weaknesses in our ministry that we might otherwise overlook.

I make a point of reading all mail addressed to me...if it is signed. I don't read anonymous mail, but if the sender will sign it, I will read it. By doing this, I have been motivated and encouraged through positive letters and cards; I have also been able to grow through the critical correspondence I have received.

People who write negative mail often have some obvious problems of their own. But sometimes they have identified a weakness or an oversight that I need to see to more powerfully communicate

COMPETITION CAN BE A PROFITABLE TOOL. IT CAN CAUSE US TO STRETCH, AND IN STRETCHING WE WILL STRENGTHEN OUR MENTAL, EMOTIONAL AND PHYSICAL MUSCLES FOR GREATER ACHIEVEMENT.

the gospel. I call this my Tuesday mail: the problem surfaces on Sunday, letters are mailed on Monday and arrive at the office on Tuesday.

Tuesday mail comes in various forms. One, of course, is the mail itself. Another might be negative comments from a survey of our visitors or congregation. The last form of Tuesday mail I will mention is the point of this section: trends of those who are leaving our church to attend another.

Sometimes groups of people leave for petty or purely personal reasons that don't communicate anything meaningful to us, but other times people leaving can communicate that we don't efficiently respond to phone calls, offer practical teaching or maintain adequate integrity in our relationships.

I understand that sometimes manipulative people try to control ministers by leaving churches. Obviously, such ungodly behavior is not what I am addressing in this chapter. Instead, what I am emphasizing is that just as quality is highlighted in both Sears and J.C. Penney stores by our shopping for the best value and the best service, so life-giving ministry can come from our desire to do what Sears and J.C. Penney have done: Grow because competition demanded that their value and service improve. In the same way, compelling ministry may be a by-product of healthy competition.

- One time I asked Dr. Cho why his church had success-fully grown to more than 80,000 cell groups. He smiled and said that they have learned to compete, in a godly way, for souls.
- Another time I asked Danny Ost, apostolic missionary to Mexico, where his passion for evangelism came from. He answered by explaining that everyone was either going to heaven or hell when they died. Because of that tension, he felt as though he were running a race against the world and the devil to win people to Christ. He was competing.

A proper response to competition causes retailers, manufacturers, phone companies, governments and yes, even churches, to do better work. Competition with one another and, in some cases, against time or "the record" makes an athlete great. And certainly, with the impor-tance of the eternal task we Christians have been given, effectiveness is a must.

So when I look at the thousands of pastors attending seminars at Willowcreek in Chicago, Saddleback in Los Angeles, First Assembly in Phoenix and Bethany World Prayer Center in Baton Rouge, it is clear: These ministers understand that the people in their communi-ties have eternal choices to make—that there is a spiritual competi-tion for them. We need to do a good job and win them to Him.

GROW TOGETHER

Communities of believers become more effective together.

Forty-four Christian leaders in Colorado Springs are currently participating in a 40-day fast. In addition, scores of leaders are doing partial fasts for 21 days, 10 days, 7 days or 3 days. Hundreds are fast-ing for one day or one meal. This is changing the countenance of our Christian community. I was at a meal two days ago where only three of the six attenders were eating. Nothing was said. It was not an issue. This discipline has become, instead, part of the Christian lifestyle in our city.

Quality in ministry prompts excellence in ministry. Once the Christians within a city choose to unite for the purpose of making it hard to go to hell from their city, they will each sense an additional responsibility to improve their own work. They will find new ways to love their city into the Kingdom. As they grow, they will improve, and the quality of the ministries will improve as the water level rises.

Because the Olympic Training Center is in Colorado Springs, we regularly see groups of cyclists training together. They train together so they can all improve through healthy competition. They must improve individually so they can improve corporately. As a result, our nation is able to form a quality team that is able to compete against other nations. Riding with excellent riders makes average athletes better.

Musicians enjoy playing with other musicians who have greater skill and experience. Why? Because when they do, they learn how to improve. Healthy competition is the primary way they grow.

Competition can be a profitable tool. It can cause us to stretch, and in stretching we will strengthen our mental, emotional and physical muscles for greater achievement. It can also awaken those of us who have been lulled to sleep by the ease of our comfort zones.

I enjoy snow skiing with people slightly better than I am. Why? So I can learn to ski with greater proficiency. Certainly, it's more comfortable for me to ski with people who cannot ski as well as I—it actually makes me look like a good skier. But if I did that all the time, my skills might erode, and I might find myself actually declining in my ability to ski.

Ministry proficiency in our cities is the same. Granted, some exceptions will occur. But most often the influences of prayer, planning and broad-based implementation of the plan will cause various ministries to try innovative approaches and, as a result, grow. As they grow, the others must make a decision. In order for all boats to rise together, each must make a positive decision to rise with the rising water.

- Some will be seaworthy, others will not.
- Some will find leaks and repair them, others will find leaks and defend them.
- Some will tune their engines by ministering to new groups in new ways, others will be satisfied with current performance.
- Some will be challenged and grow from the strengths of their neighboring churches. Others will prefer the safety of mediocrity and compromise.

- Some will enjoy rechecking their navigation by praying and talking with others. Others will prefer their own exclusive expertise.
- Some will come to the right conclusions because of the need for life-giving churches to grow. Others will never understand and actually believe that if their own boat rises, that's enough.
- Some will be successful for eternal causes. A few will not.
- Some will cause the water to rise and other boats to rise with it. Others will not influence the water at all.

We have no choice. The depravity of our society and the finality of heaven and hell require that we raise the water level in every city in our nation. In so doing, we must do everything within our power to raise the water level of the Holy Spirit's activity so that life-giving churches throughout our city grow. It can be done. It must be done. It will be done. As we:

Pray together.
Plan together.
Go together.
Grow together.

Now.

Note:
1. Ted Haggard, *Primary Purpose* (Lake Mary, FL: Creation House, 1995), pp. 76-88.

GROW TOGETHER

CREATING BROAD-BASED CHURCH GROWTH
BY TED HAGGARD

TED HAGGARD

HARD QUESTIONS ANSWERED

As groups of Christian leaders build coalitions to enhance evangelism, a number of questions are being asked. This chapter provides a compilation of some of the more pertinent questions and their answers.

Q. Why must we network together?

A. Networks make us more effective if done correctly. They are relationships that allow us to benefit from the experiences and resources of others, so we can grow at the same time—through conversion growth.

Q. I am not an influential leader, but I know this approach is the greatest hope for our community. What can I do?

A. This may sound self-serving, but distribute copies of this book, *Primary Purpose* (Creation House) and *That None Should Perish* (Regal) among the Christian leaders in your community. As you do, the seeds of partnerships will begin to take root in their thinking, and partnerships will naturally begin to develop.

Q. Who needs to be the initiator?

A. If you have the ability to convene leaders at all, you need to be the initiator. If you are in a positive relationship with someone who has a stronger ability to convene leadership, encourage that person. Because you have a vision for the Body of Christ to work together more effectively in reaching the lost, you must take action. But remember, most people will only know what you are doing if you provide them with the material to explain it. Because of the way we used to structure pastors' meetings, they will assume you are starting a ministerial alliance. So it is important that you seed copies of the previously mentioned books among people in your city. If you want people to receive from you, be sure to approach them from a servant's point of view. Never give this book to another with a highbrowed "you need this." Instead, give it saying it was a blessing to you, and that you think it might be a blessing to the one who is receiving it. Buy the person a copy to keep, that way he or she can read it at leisure.

Q. What is the criteria for the city or regional coordinator?

A. The coordinator may be any well-respected Christian leader. I believe it is easier if a servant-ministry person can be utilized who is respected in his or her own local church; but most cities use pastors or well-liked lay-men. The coordinator needs to be:

- Well respected in the community;
- A person who carries and presents himself or her-self honorably;
- A person who possesses and practices personal integrity;
- One who meets the biblical qualifications for eldership;
- Someone who is willing to follow the lead of the churches and balance infusing them with fresh ideas;
- A person with enough backbone to keep things moving in unity, but not arrogant or haughty;
- One who would never appoint himself or herself;
- Someone who has lived in the city at least 10 years with a good reputation among those who know him or her;
- A man or woman who avoids church/pastoral/ser-vant-ministry moods or quibbles. Someone the lead-ers listen to, but one who does not talk too much. A good listener, yet a quality speaker;
- Someone who laughs easily.

Q. A man came to my office who said he was called to our city to bring harmony to the churches. Even though he is new in town, he seems to be a wonderful man and, after all, he moved here because of the call. Do you think he is the right one?

A. No. Absolutely not! He should not even be a consider-ation. He may be a great catalyst for what God wants to do, but he can't be the point person. A basic rule is: Never, ever allow your city coordinator be a self-appointed person who is new in town. Your coordina-tor needs to be known by some people in your com-munity. Relationships take time, and partnerships are formed through relationships.

Q.   How should we identify absolutes, and show how
they work to protect the movement?

A.   In *Primary Purpose* I [Ted Haggard] say that absolutes
are what the Bible actually says. Read it and stop.

UNITY ALONE IS NOT POWER, BUT PURPOSE POWERED BY UNITY IS UNSTOPPABLE.

Those are the absolutes. But here in Colorado Springs,
The Net says that the absolutes are twofold: (1) "We
believe that the Bible is our sole source of authority for
faith and practice." And (2) "We believe in the person
and works of Jesus Christ: Fully God, Fully Man, For
full salvation as Lord and Savior." This works well.

Q   What is the purpose of this group of churches?

A.   To glorify God and evangelize the lost. In John 17,
Jesus prayed that we might be one so that the world
might believe. In that prayer, Jesus forever linked the
relationship between unity and evangelism. So, we
know that as a unified Body, we have a greater potential for effectively evangelizing our community than if
we are fragmented. However, we must not assume
that we are automatically more effective at evangelism
because we are unified. That is not the case. As a matter of fact, occasionally in the midst of unity, some of
our greatest evangelistic churches loose their cutting
edge in an attempt to "get along." Unity alone is not
power, but purpose powered by unity is unstoppable.

Q. What about the local Council or Ministerial Association that has been in the community for a long time?

A. In some places the Council of Churches or Ministerial Association may be a good place to develop a prayer movement among the pastors. In many cities these groups have become passive, routine fellowship meetings. They do have value, but generally don't facilitate growth. This may be a great place to start the "pray together" function. Through these prayer times, they will determine whether it is best to renew and revitalize the Council of Churches or Ministerial Association to focus on a strategic movement to reach the city for Christ or to form a new entity.

Q. What should we as a coalition of churches do about the pressing political issues of the day? How involved should we be?

A. Our purpose is evangelism and the promotion of the gospel. That purpose needs to be firmly established in everyone's mind. Once that is done, you will receive great opportunities within the non-Christian community. But if you become a political entity, many open doors will close. If you chose to become politically involved as a coalition, you should limit your involvement to providing information about chosen issues. It is commendable for the coalition to be a moral voice in the community, but be careful to always speak from the position of wanting to help and serve people.

Q. I pastor a large church, but the man putting the coalition of churches together pastors a small church that, in my view, will never grow. I do not respect this brother very much, but because he is the initiator of this group, I must work with some of his bad ideas. What should I do?

A. Be careful. We both know that humility can only be identified as it is lived out before us. People can't just *be* humble. Inherent in humility is the recognition of others—that we need each other to accomplish the calling God has given us in our cities. It is better to grow together than to grow alone. Prayerlessness, lack of devotion to the Scriptures and a failure to recognize our need for others are all rooted in the same sin: Pride. Once you build a relationship with this brother by participating in the network, he will glean from some of your good ideas—as long as both of you are humble. Then, both of your churches have a greater potential for growth.

Q. But I don't need him. His church is the size of some of my smaller departments.

A. That may be true, but you need his "department" to be successful, and he needs your group of departments to be successful. If you both want to impact your city by growing through conversion growth—you need each other. It is honorable to acknowledge that we cannot change our cities by ourselves—we need the group. The whole city will not be reached through our individual ministries. A humble spirit is required for the small church pastor to work with the larger churches, just as humility is necessary in the larger churches to value the smaller ones. Humility cuts both ways; thus we've got to allow the Holy Spirit to guide our actions and interactions with humility.

Q. I don't think you get it. I don't believe I need them. I don't like them, nor do I have time for them. I can do more for the gospel alone.

A. I know you really believe that, and I would agree with you if you were right. Agreed, it does appear that you can do more alone. But God did not create the Body to function that way. We need each other whether we see it or not. I have five children. My oldest two probably do not vividly see their need for their younger brothers. But as their dad, I can see them each refining the other's character. A mall needs the anchor stores, and the smaller vendors. Only together do they make a prosperous mall. Cities need anchor churches and smaller churches as well—as long as they are life-giving and growing.

Q. What is the role of the network when one of the pastors falls into sin in the city?

A. Issues of discipline are the primary responsibility of each local church, and its own church government. The responsibility of the coordinator for the network of churches is to bring any potential problems to the attention of the one suspected of falling into sin. Then, if that pastor has fallen, to confront the pastor privately. The network of churches should then disassociate from that one church until the situation has been remedied. The role of the network is not to expose, discipline or involve itself with the internal working of any church. It is, however, the role of the network to associate itself with pastors and churches that have integrity.

Q. Do you have any unusual agreements with your city coordinator that relate to the "sin" issue?

A. Yes. Sometimes we do things in our churches that offend people without our knowledge. Because Jaan is out in the community as the coordinator, people will tell him things they would never say to me. I have asked him to tell me if he should hear anything negative about me of substance—that is, something I should repent for or correct. I have also told him I do not need to hear random rumors, subjective opinions, etc. But if I have sinned against my brother or sister, I want to know it and fix it.

Q. You seem to think that if the city coordinator is not a

pastor, the person should be highly committed and involved in one local church. That would be disaster in my city. Shouldn't the coordinator be visiting all of the local churches rather than being committed to one local church?

A. No. In this generation all of us need to have the same group of people, week after week, that we meet with for worship and growth in His Word. It is true, the coordinator should visit other churches. But he or she should also be firmly committed to one church, and be well respected there. The person needs to have a pastor and have personal involvement in ministry through his or her own local church.

Q. My denomination has its own community group. Why do I need this one, too?

A. Because your denominational group is probably too narrow. Partnership and strategic thinking was birthed by the National Association of Evangelicals and has been developed by Mission America. Therefore, your denominational leadership is probably aware and supportive of developing city strategies. So I would encourage your denominational group to network with other life-giving groups and develop strategies for reaching your city. With a little communication, your effectiveness can increase dramatically.

Q. Is this going to cost me money?

A. Probably not. If anything, it will cause the money you are currently spending to produce more. Here in Colorado Springs, we have a community coordinator and an office, so local churches provide monthly support. But most cities use a pastor or community leader who is paid by another organization and already has offices. That works well, too.

Q. Isn't it easier to be exclusive rather than inclusive?

A. Yes, but exclusivity within the Body of Christ is not effective—it's counterproductive. It limits us. It sends people to hell.

Q. What am I going to have to give up theologically to work with these guys?

A. Nothing theologically, unless your doctrine of sanctification causes you to believe that only you and your group are true Christians. But most of us have come to understand that various Bible-believing Christian groups believe what they believe for good reasons. All of us loose a little of our exclusivity and high-mindedness when we meet people from another group, and discover that they, too, are committed Christians. Please understand, when we talk about coalitions, we are talking about life-giving, Bible-believing, born-again believers who value the Scriptures and love the Lord Jesus Christ. We are not encouraging liberal, ecumenical meetings of the "community of faith." Orthodox, fundamental Christianity is our common ground.

Q. Aren't the guys who participate in these types of meetings the losers—the "wanna be's"? My church is successful, and I'm already too busy. My observation is that the small church leaders want to meet and strategize, but the big church guys don't.

A. Yes, in many cities this is true. The problem is, though, that as the "wanna be's" do this, many of them become what they wanna be—effective and influential ministries to the city. I have learned that every few years the most effective ministries in any community switch roles in relationship to others. In Colorado Springs, more than half of the largest churches in town are relatively new churches that partnership together. In many cities, the leading churches of 15 years ago are no longer important. To be productive today is important, but it is even better to position your ministry in the flow of what God is doing citywide so you will be productive tomorrow, too.

Q.   Is this a support group?

A.   Sometimes it is, but that's not our primary role. The group is comprised of its own unique components. Each city needs to establish its own group parameters. In our city, the prayer groups are strong support

SWITCH FROM A SHORTAGE MENTALITY TO AN ABUNDANCE MENTALITY; MAKE THE POND BIGGER!

groups, but when The Net meets, it meets to work. It is the strategic planning group.

Q.   In one sentence, what are these groups?

A.   These groups are local church-based strategic partnerships for evangelism.

Q.   Many people say churches are not supposed to compete, but we do. Comparisons do exist and, bottom line, people go to either our church or to the other guy's church. It *is* competition to increase our own church's attendance. If our church doesn't grow, I'm in trouble. And the easiest way to make it grow is to attract Christians. Can we grow without competing?

A.   I hear you and certainly sympathize with what you are saying. People remind us of this truth every time they leave our church for another, or come to our church from another one because "ours is better." The big decision, though, is how we choose our response. Certainly we need to be faithful to effectively minister to people, but we must minister with the intention of increasing the pool of people citywide attending life-giving churches. Switch from a shortage mentality to an abundance mentality; make the pond bigger! That will provide more people for everyone. Notice that a shortage of lost people has never existed, only a shortage of believers. So, don't be possessive of the Christians. Simply minister to others, keeping the lost in mind. That way everyone can grow.

Q. I pastor a small church and enjoy getting together with larger church pastors, but many times they are so dominant. How should I respond?

A. Respond with an open mind and heart. Leadership meetings are great opportunities to hear a variety of new ideas. It is good to hear the values, disciplines and hearts of larger-church pastors. You will learn more in informal conversation than in a month of sermons from them. They usually speak openly in these meetings. You may want to adopt some of their ideas; others you will discard. But hearing from leaders of larger churches can help all of us grow in our abilities to minister to people.

Q. I can see the purpose for the big churches getting together to plan strategy, but why should the little churches be involved?

A. These meetings force everyone to learn, to stretch, to grow and to get focused. These groups can give smaller-church leaders purpose and the relationships necessary to undergird them as they grow in ministry. For the smaller-church leaders, these groups have no negatives.

Q. I don't need the relational, support-group atmosphere. What does this have to do with evangelism?

A. Of all the various types of evangelism that we do, the highest percentage of people who come to Christ and become planted in churches are those who come to Christ because of a friend who then disciples them in a local church. Relationships are the key to "retaining the harvest." So, Christian leaders must understand long-term, healthy relationships. As Christian leaders learn these skills among other leaders, it is easier for them to instruct their churches in effective friendship evangelism.

Q. Some studies have suggested that churches are generally horrible at evangelism. Why do you believe our getting together will increase our ability to evangelize?

A. Because you're not getting together to get together; you're meeting to establish focus and purpose. You are right, we have no reason to believe that just because leaders are getting together and developing harmony, people will come to Christ in greater number. But that harmony does open the door for specific, purposeful local-church-based strategies to be developed for evangelism. Our compelling purpose causes the creative resources of local churches to be directed toward the lost instead of themselves, which in turn causes an increase in evangelism.

Q. Is this effort leading us to sponsor evangelistic efforts and unified evangelistic events?

A. No, our goal is not to create a forum to sponsor additional events. Our goal is to cause churches to work strategically in a coordinated fashion so they will grow and become increasingly effective.

Q. Then how will this facilitate evangelism?

A. Local churches are the containers of the harvest. They disciple people. In addition, they have remarkable resilience and the resources to reach people in their own communities and cultures. They always grow when given spiritual renewal and purpose outside themselves. Church growth is no mystery. Our goal, though, is to apply some of the principles we know about church growth to the churches citywide.

Q. Why is this better?

A. Because local church-based evangelism retains the harvest much better than any other kind of evangelism. Local church-based evangelism is the most effective kind of evangelism that we know of to transform cities. We are supportive of all Christian evangelism, but we already have the resources to do this.

Q. What is the role of the servant ministries?

A. Servant ministries form because they have an area of expertise that is purposeful, focused and effective. So when local churches partner with servant ministries, the combination works well. When we combine the family relationships of a local church with the resources and expertise of servant ministries, the outreach potential is enormous.

Q. What does it mean to say, "local church-based evangelism"?

A. Evangelism that happens in or through a local church or a group of local churches. I measure the effectiveness of prayer and evangelism by their impact upon the local church. So when Christian leaders come together to share information, to strategize and to purposefully build relationships for evangelism, the local church should be strengthened. Note: They are not getting together to do evangelism, but to strategize for evangelism through their churches.

Q.   We all have our own ideas about the forms of evangelism we believe are the most effective. How do we work together?

A.   Without coordinated efforts, individual churches cannot do thorough evangelism. They can focus on their own spheres of influence, which means they won't reach a broad enough group within their city. So many times they revert to growth through transfer growth, appealing to other Christians who are usually members of, or somewhat affiliated with, other local churches. In addition, if a group gets together, and in the name of unity sponsors a citywide evangelistic meeting, statistics prove that this kind of effort costs a huge amount of money and often does not produce growth in local churches. But in this book, we are emphasizing that each church can reach people within its own sphere of influence doing what it does best as a church, while being coordinated within the whole Body in the city. This works best.

Q.   Does this work in every city, regardless of population?

A.   Because we are talking about praying together, planning together, going together and growing together— yes, that outline works in every city. The prayers will vary from city to city because of spiritual differences. Obviously, the strategies will vary. The personalities of the churches will cause the implementation of the strategies to look different, but the net result—growth in most of the life-giving churches of the city—will be the same.

Q.   I like the idea, but I don't like the way it is being approached in my city. What can I do?

A.   Anytime a majority of pastors in a city become motivated to work together, others should sit up and take notice. Even if it is not done exactly the way you would like it, the fact that there is a broad-based movement to do something demands your participation and support. Something is better than nothing. Don't be confused by style-over-substance issues. Get on board and encourage the vision of targeting and reaching your city.

Q.   I am pleased with the size of my church. Should I still be involved?

A.   The statistics speak too loudly for us to ignore. Regardless of how satisfied you are with your church's membership or budget, the real questions are: How do we compare to our city as a whole? What percentage of teenagers are believers in your city? What percentage of singles are Christians in your city? How many business professionals in your city know the Lord? We must be persuaded by the *facts* of our city! We cannot become self-satisfied in our own world, pretending the lost of our cities don't exist. We should never be deceived by our own perceived success; but instead, we should work together for the bigger purpose of the success of the kingdom of God within our cities.

Q.   Why wasn't there much discussion about this 50 years ago?

A.   In the United States, we have just discovered the effectiveness of broad-based strategic alliances. For the last 50 years, the National Association of Evangelicals has built an infrastructure of harmony that Mission America and others are currently building upon for the purpose of increasingly effective evangelistic efforts. Not only are broad-based alliances between Christian churches increasingly possible, but now partnerships between local churches and servant ministries are also becoming easy to construct. The servant ministries now publicly position themselves as the support and resource structure to supplement the efforts of proactive local churches. With huge populations gathering in cities, strategic alliances between churches and the accompanying partnerships with servant ministries offer an unparalleled opportunity for the Body of Christ to communicate the gospel to the people of large population centers.

EARN THE RIGHT TO BE HEARD THROUGH SERVING OTHERS, AND SEEK GOD FOR WISDOM IN THE AREA OF SPIRITUAL AUTHORITY.

Q. Why do you think the people involved should have the "authority to convene"? What does that mean?

A. In Christian circles the "authority to convene" indicates spiritual authority. John Maxwell says, "He who leads with no one following is only taking a walk." Many pastors today want to lead in their cities, but have not recognized their need for God's dispensation of spiritual authority for the task. Spread the material and cooperate. Do all that you can do within your own circle of influence and allow God to add people with even more influence. Give them space to work. As this process continues, the result will be a citywide partnership that will make it hard to go to hell from your city. And the Church will then be known for "loving your city into the Kingdom."

Q. I believe strongly in this, but I can't get others to do it with me. They are consumed in what they are doing now. What should I do?

A. Earn the right to be heard through serving others, and

seek God for wisdom in the area of spiritual authority. Something wonderful happens when you let your actions speak for you. Others will begin to develop trust in you because you've been a stable, steady, encouraging influence in your city. Obviously, this requires time and patience, but self-appointed leaders rarely convince others to follow them for long.

A few weeks ago, I was being interviewed at a local radio station by a gentleman who two years earlier had visited my office to discuss several things he felt as though the Lord had laid on his heart. I encouraged him in that meeting to do nothing for at least two years. That day at the radio station, he proceeded to tell me how every one of those ideas were going to be so easy now that he had developed trust and a good reputation in the city, whereas two years earlier, they would have been much more difficult. He had earned the right to be heard.

Q. Do you think prayer and fasting would help me?

A. Maybe. It depends upon how open you are. But I know of no greater spiritual discipline for allowing God to increase your spiritual authority to lead, both in your church and your city. Somehow, the Lord works within us during a fast to break us down, and then build us back up again. Consecration of our motives, our attitudes and our secret sins create a rich environment where God can place His desires in us, purifying, refining and shaping us into His vessels.

Dr. David Yonggi Cho is the most vocal proponent of a lifestyle of prayer and fasting for effective ministry. Every day on Prayer Mountain in Seoul, Korea, thousands of people are praying and fasting as a result of Dr. Cho's teaching and training. His life and ministry point to the fact that as you pray and fast, the Lord will place His vision in you and grow your spiritual authority to carry out that vision. And the most convincing factor that prayer and fasting works? The largest church in the world!

Q. I believe I do have the spiritual authority. God gave it to me. But the other leaders in the city will not respond to me.

A. Unfortunately, the only way to know if we have spiritual authority in our lives is by the confirmation of other believers. God gives us the opportunity to lead and speak into the lives of others, and only when they respond, do we have the confirmation that God has indeed given us His spiritual authority. If spiritual authority is not apparent in your ministry, then keep asking God to grant His grace in your life to grow in it. When He grants it...you'll know.

 I still remember the day I was praying in the basement of my house when the Lord impressed upon me that He had given me the spiritual authority to pastor 75 people. And sure enough, our attendance bubbled to 75 or so people. Then I began to sense the Lord wanted us to grow to 150, but I needed the spiritual authority to pastor them. I asked Him and He granted it. Again, it happened with 300—then 700—then 1,500, 3,000 and now 6,000. Every time as God granted the spiritual authority, our attendance grew and would level off. It was during this time I realized the significance of asking the Lord to grant His spiritual authority in my life and ministry. In addition, I began to understand that as God grants it, we don't need to say it to anyone. He supernaturally confirms it through the response of others.

Q. What should I do while I wait?

A. Don't wait—start loving your city into the Kingdom!

10

SEEKING THE CITY'S PEACE

IT CAN BE DONE!

BY JACK W. HAYFORD

JACK W. HAYFORD

"Please remove my name from your mailing list! I don't 'love Los Angeles,' and I don't have time for your prayer meeting!"

It sounded pretty grim.

The card that came to my desk [Jack Hayford] was hardly encouraging. We had sent our invitations to as many pastors as possible, and heard little response. We hoped this was not representative! The "Initiating Committee," as we called ourselves, consisted of a broad-based team of Los Angeles's spiritual leaders who had been praying together for months. This band of leaders was now taking steps we had not earlier anticipated. We collectively felt a larger gathering would be the mind of the Spirit, but was this our idea or His?

We had set the date to assure that at least all of us could be present (see chapter 1). By a peculiarity we all sensed to be an act of providence, Tuesday, February 14, 1989, turned out to be the best—Valentine's Day! Because God's love had so constrained and bonded us all from the beginning, it made sense:

God's love for our city was the fountainhead.

Now, as we searched for a name to give our event, two priorities motivated us: (1) seeking pastoral unity; (2) focusing prayer for our city. They were clear in our vision and—we all believed—were to be kept as priorities...and in that order; relationship, then intercession.

SHEPHERDS LOVE L.A.

We chose the phrase, Shepherds LOVE L.A., first because we were not merely seeking to generate a general crowd of interested Christians. We wanted to gather spiritual leaders from the broader circle of the Church in our city. Second, we were moved by a verse of Scripture.

> Seek the peace of the city where I have caused you to be carried away captive, and pray to the Lord for it; for in its peace you will have peace (Jer. 29:7, *NKJV*).

During one of the first gatherings of our smaller group Lloyd Ogilvie had referenced this text. His remarks were especially moving to me, for they summarized the essence of something I had been feeling with increasing conviction. After observing the background of Jeremiah's words to those who were being exiled to Babylon, Lloyd noted the parallels to our situation as spiritual leaders, notwithstanding obvious factors in the historic context that did not apply.

1. We all had in common a divine placement in a city dominated by a pagan mind-set.
2. We all were hearing a prophetic call to pray to God for the "peace" (i.e., the well-being) of our city.
3. We could all see the promise that if we would do this, we would find our own sense of "peace."

Somehow, Lloyd's sharing these insights brought a boldness that permitted me to relate a picture that had been impressed on my spirit a few days before. I saw a great gathering of people—pastors, nearly filling Hollywood Presbyterian Church. As I shared this, an electric unity was evidenced. All the men agreed this was something we should pursue. And Lloyd gladly offered to seek the clearance of his elders for the date, which was quickly decided as I have previously mentioned. What would happen? Would that one terse, anguished response—"I don't love L.A.!"—be the answer?

An Overwhelming Beginning

Instead, the crowd stunned us all! We were jubilant! Some said 1,000 were present, including deacons, elders and pastoral assistants. More likely the number was closer to 700, but the scope of leaders in attendance and the hundreds of different congregations represented was incredibly gratifying. It had not come about easily, however.

The practical pursuit of the gathering involved the handling of considerable communication problems in a town such as ours, but these steps lent to an effective beginning:

- We worked hard and made an investment in compiling a mailing list of as many churches as possible. With at least 5,000 in Los Angeles, and no master list whatsoever in existence, we sought to get word to everyone.
- Thousands of congregations in Los Angeles are either non-English speaking or non-evangelical. We did not know what response we might have, but we were diligent in our attempt to see that every spiritual shepherd in our city was at least made aware. We wanted to preempt any "elitist" notions.
- Each of us (the Initiating Committee) did our best to motivate our own constituencies. For example, I urged Los Angeles pastors in my denomination (Foursquare) to make every effort to come. Other representative men did the same in their movements.
- Two mailings were sent—6 weeks in advance, then

again 10 days before the event—to explain the concept
prompting our gathering, and to outline the content of
the event. A few of us also secured the help of congregational elders who made personal, confidential
phone calls of invitation to pastors whose names were
provided on a list for them.

- We arranged a lite-breakfast-on-arrival welcome for
all who came, knowing this would help secure closer
to an on-time appearance (7 A.M.). We also believed
the fellowship over coffee, fruit and rolls, the elders of
Hollywood Presbyterian Church were gracious to
serve us, would help meeting, interaction and cama-
raderie.

All of these factors contributed to a marvelous morning, a great
beginning and a continuing miracle of grace that extends to the present, seven years later. While the harsh letter of protest might have
caused a moment's doubt, it later moved us to a greater sense of
regret and love for a beleaguered shepherd who apparently was sinking in some pool of despondency. That one response proved, to our
view, the need for our "shepherd" emphasis as the distinctive of
LOVE L.A.

GUIDING CONCEPTS

Many outstanding prayer movements today have a special place in
advancing Christ's purpose in His Church across our nation. Our
"call" to pastor-leadership-at-prayer, came when this prayer awakening was just beginning to stir blessing in the Body of Christ. With
this environment, we felt assured of a crowd if (1) we issued an open
invitation to all believers, and (2) made a public pursuit of media
publicity in spreading the word. Instead, however, we did neither.

First, we felt called to specifically seek the bonding of pastors; to
weld leaders together in prayer. Ironically, this is the most difficult
group to gain trust with, especially in the midst of Los Angeles's "distance" factors outlined in chapter 1. Second, though most of us had a
favorable entree to the religion editors at both the *Los Angeles Times*
and the *Daily News*, we kept this a low-profile event. We had a reason.

From its inception, Shepherds LOVE L.A. has had a relational focus almost greater than an intercessory one. This may strike some readers as less than spiritual, but let me explain. Our goal was to build trust between leaders. We were convinced that a genuinely

A GENUINELY DYNAMIC PRAYER FELLOWSHIP WOULD NOT ONLY REQUIRE MUTUAL TRUST AS A BEGINNING POINT, BUT IT WOULD ALSO MULTIPLY PRAYER.

dynamic prayer fellowship would not only require mutual trust as a beginning point, but that it would also multiply prayer. This is exactly what happened, and it can be described in its process as well as demonstrated in its fruitfulness.

1. The Process
The conduct of our Shepherds LOVE L.A. gatherings is unbelievably simple. Primary components are:

a. A traditional hymn of praise and one or two contemporary choruses open. All that follows involves a variety of participants and a minimum of program steerage.

b. An extended (1 to 2 full minutes) of greeting follows a brief invocation; urging those present to move around in reaching out to others.

c. A 5- to 8-minute time of private, personal prayer is introduced, calling and allowing those present to quietly kneel and present themselves, their day and our meeting to the Lord. The preparation of our hearts for the rest of the prayer meeting is enjoined.

d. A brief series of worship choruses or an appropriate hymn concludes this segment.

e. One of the Initiating Team brings a 12- to 15-minute, self-disclosing devotional thought—geared to model vulnerability of ourselves as brothers and sisters with one another. (We avoid the sermonic or the didactic: This is "hear my heart" time.)

f. The first of three times of group prayer occurs: Number one is a 20- to 30-minute time when all present break into groups of four or five . The objective is to relate person-to-person, honest-to-God. We discourage "ministry"-focused requests (i.e., what I do). Instead we encourage opening heart-to-heart regarding "what's really most on my mind, and what I'm struggling with right now." Admittedly, this focus is not always easy to secure, but we've found great, great gain in fostering true-hearted communion with one another. We have also discovered the blessing of an atmosphere that begets deep trust and strong, follow-through friendships.

g. Another set of worship choruses transitions us to our number two time of group prayer. Usually, the same group (four to five) reconvenes, but this time for only 10-12 minutes. The focus: Our church, our congregation, our ministry program, our work.

h. This time concludes with a brief summary of "business" regarding Shepherds LOVE L.A.: (i) attendance is registered on cards; (ii) announcement is made regarding next meeting (quarterly); (iii) acknowledgment is given to any citywide ministry situation potentially involving us all. We are insistent that local congregational events not be promoted, but the following are examples of what we do announce: Area-wide crusades (Luis Palau, Greg Laurie, Promise Keepers, T. D. Jakes), our local Mayor's Prayer Breakfast, area Concerts of Prayer or March for Jesus.

NOTE: We do not generally receive an offering for our ministry costs. We ask any who wish information about how their congregations can share to indicate this on the registration card. A simple follow-up letter is then sent, explaining how to give. The account is monitored by the Initiating Committee and maintained in the business affairs of a designated committee member's church.

HIGHLIGHT INTERCESSION

The third (number three) and final season of prayer at each Shepherds LOVE L.A. gathering is a highlighted time of intercession. This part of the meeting stirs and releases a holy and dynamic agreement, and we are unafraid of emotion, remembering "the effectual fervent prayer of a righteous man avails much" (Jas. 5:16, *NKJV*).

It's a risky period in the prayer gathering, because of this. The leadership has been faced with some delicate situations on occasion, as microphones are opened in the aisles and anyone present is welcomed to come and lead the group. We have not been disappointed.

Most of the time nothing is said that would bother any person of passion in prayer, but a much-needed emphasis is maintained on two things—tolerance and brevity. Some prayers express opinions or are motivated by doctrinal viewpoints that may not be shared by everyone present, but we allow "space" for hearts to cry out to God. Furthermore, expecting brevity of expression among a band of pastors is like expecting the sunrise to wait! Nonetheless, these challenges pale before the larger blessings we continually realize in the prayer fellowship.

Occasionally this season of the prayer meeting has included unscheduled exhortations, as a brother or sister asks to precede their prayer with an explanation or a motivating remark. We allow this— and we've profited far more than been penalized for this decision. The Shepherds LOVE L.A. leadership has avoided planning this segment so tightly that little room exists for spontaneous dealings of the Spirit as He moves on the pastors who are present.

A powerfully moving occurrence, which has now become a regular part of the intercessory agenda, took place at an early gathering. Lloyd Ogilvie suggested, "Let's have anyone here whose native language or mother tongue is other than English, lead us by praying in that language." Within 25 minutes, intercession had been offered in more than 15 languages, and there wasn't a dry eye in the place.

"Strange," commented Bishop Ken Ulmer, pastor of Faithful Central Missionary Baptist, and today a part of the Initiating Committee: "It's strange how clearly the 'spirit' of what is being prayed comes through to our understanding, even though we don't know the words."

This innovation in our prayer time, possibly more than any other single thing, illustrates the blend of diversity and the blessings of unity born through Shepherds LOVE L.A. That is, except for one: we have become ONE.

ANSWERED PRAYER [IS] THE FIRST TEST OF A PRAYER MEETING'S EFFECTIVENESS.

2. The Fruitfulness

The fruit of Shepherds LOVE L.A. is manifest in how its variety, its multiplicity and its durability has processed to a beautiful unity among participants. This has come about as God has done many things to verify the value of our gatherings.

First, it is understandable that answered prayer would be the first test of a prayer meeting's effectiveness. However, by that measure, some outside observer might wonder if anyone has been praying in Los Angeles at all, given its past few years of trauma! Fires, floods, a historic riot and a devastating earthquake have scarred the face of the city in the eyes of most beholders. Nonetheless, inside the circle of our town's spiritual leadership, a steady flow of praise has been rising amid and beyond these disasters.

Second, that first value is explainable because of the personal and relational transformation we have realized. A closer bond—a knit of genuine brotherly love—has developed between many leaders because of having prayer heart-to-heart, "struggling-thru'-the-stuff" prayer with one another. This has manifest in the voluntary planning of many interchurch events—churches gathering together, joining in worship. These events reflect at many local congregations' corporate levels what has begun at personal dimensions with their pastors.

Dozens of cases of these smaller events exist, but we also had a pair of climactic happenings. Two grand gatherings involving more than 50 congregations each time have taken place at Crenshaw Christian Center during the past five year, with nearly 10,000 in attendance at the largest. The most remarkable feature in these gatherings, aside form the great volume of prayer going forth for the city, was the large attendance of suburban whites who traveled to an inner city Black congregation's site to fellowship...at night!!

A SMALL BUT GREAT SUM

Has "peace" come to the city? Not quite—not yet. But undeniably great changes have occurred that signal a turn in the flow of things spiritual from where they have been throughout the preceding 25 years. A small but great sum is revealed when a tally of results is even attempted:

- Cooperation unknown and apparently unavailable among churches for decades has been learned. Luis Palau's crusade (June 1-5, 1994) in the San Fernando Valley area of the city found participation by more than 175 congregations. At the time of this writing, Greg Laurie's team is finding response warranting a crusade planned for the near future.
- The banded-together intercession of Los Angeles's shepherds, carried home to their congregations, is the only possible explanation for the dramatic reduction in gang violence and street warring in the city. Newspapers report the reduced bloodshed, but have little ability to provide understanding of the deeper dimension of breakthrough that has brought this victory to Los Angeles.
- Two mayors, Tom Bradley and Richard Riordan, have both risen repeatedly to commend the pastoral leadership of the city. They know firsthand that apart from the united response of these leaders, the aftermath of the riots and the earthquake would have been a less hope-filled story of recovery. And we—the pastors—know that except for the relationship we have gained through Shepherds LOVE L.A., no such united response would have occurred. God, by His Spirit, and in sovereign precognition of these disasters, forged a bond between a diverse Body and separated shepherds, and prepared us for the season of trial our city has traversed.

LINCOLN CHRISTIAN COLLEGE AND SEMINARY

With this, an outside observer might wonder why Shepherds LOVE L.A. usually hosts an average of 200 to 300 pastor-leaders each time we gather these days (only 200!). But multiplicity—i.e., "multiplying"—has taken place. From the onset, our prayer gathering has sought to ignite the formation of area groups within the more immediate and approximate locations of each pastor's parish. So, while our larger gatherings are smaller than the first, a significant number of communities within the massive and widely spread metropolis now have more accessible pastoral prayer gatherings. Many of these claim LOVE L.A. as their parent—and the beat goes on.

How long will it last? We don't know. But we do know we tried to stop it once and couldn't. We were ready after five years to ask, "Are we through?"

John Dawson put it well in summing up the consensus: "This prayer meeting was born for an hour that has not yet run its course." So we continue.

Shepherds LOVE L.A. may not be a model for everyone, but hundreds of Los Angeles's area pastors call it a miracle: "It's the Lord's doing, and it is marvelous in our eyes!"

3 4711 00148 3025